Jack K[...]e
younge[...] e at-
tended [...] chol-
arship [...] met
Neal Cassady, Allen Ginsberg, and [...] He quit
school in his sophomore year and joined the Merchant Marine, be-
ginning the restless wanderings that were to continue for the greater
part of his life. His first novel, *The Town and the City*, appeared in
1950, but it was *On the Road*, first published in 1957 and memo-
rializing his adventures with Neal Cassady, that epitomized to the
world what became known as the "Beat generation" and made Ker-
ouac one of the most controversial and best-known writers of his
time. Publication of his many other books followed, among them
The Dharma Bums, *The Subterraneans*, and *Big Sur*. Kerouac con-
sidered them all to be part of The Duluoz Legend. "In my old age,"
he wrote, "I intend to collect all my work and reinsert my pantheon
of uniform names, leave the long shelf full of books there, and die
happy." He died in St. Petersburg, Florida, in 1969, at the age of
forty-seven.

By Jack Kerouac

THE TOWN AND THE CITY

ON THE ROAD

THE DHARMA BUMS

THE SUBTERRANEANS

DOCTOR SAX

MAGGIE CASSIDY

MEXICO CITY BLUES

THE SCRIPTURE OF THE GOLDEN ETERNITY

TRISTESSA

LONESOME TRAVELER

BOOK OF DREAMS

PULL MY DAISY

BIG SUR

VISIONS OF GERARD

DESOLATION ANGELS

SATORI IN PARIS

VANITY OF DULUOZ

SCATTERED POEMS

PIC

VISIONS OF CODY

HEAVEN AND OTHER POEMS

POMES ALL SIZES

OLD ANGEL MIDNIGHT

GOOD BLONDE & OTHERS

THE PORTABLE JACK KEROUAC

SELECTED LETTERS: 1940–1956

BOOK OF BLUES

JACK KEROUAC

BOOK OF
BLUES

PENGUIN POETS

PENGUIN BOOKS
Published by the Penguin Group
Penguin Books USA Inc., 375 Hudson Street, New York, New York 10014, U.S.A.
Penguin Books Ltd, 27 Wrights Lane, London W8 5TZ, England
Penguin Books Australia Ltd, Ringwood, Victoria, Australia
Penguin Books Canada Ltd, 10 Alcorn Avenue, Toronto, Ontario, Canada M4V 3B2
Penguin Books (N.Z.) Ltd, 182–190 Wairau Road, Auckland 10, New Zealand

Penguin Books Ltd, Registered Offices:
Harmondsworth, Middlesex, England

First published in Penguin Books 1995

1   3   5   7   9   10   8   6   4   2

Grateful acknowledgment is made for permission to reprint the following copyrighted works:
Selection from *Jack Kerouac* by Tom Clark. Copyright © 1984 by Tom Clark.
By permission of Marlowe & Company.
Selection from "Statement on Poetics for *The New American Poetry*"
from *Good Blonde & Others* by Jack Kerouac. © 1993, by permission of Grey Fox Press.
Selection from *Understanding the Beats* by Edward Halsey Foster.
By permission of the University of South Carolina Press.
"Jack Would Speak Through the Imperfect Medium of Alice" from *Selected
Poems of Alice Notley*, Talisman House, Publishers, 1993. Reprinted by
permission of the publisher. Copyright © 1993 by Alice Notley.

LIBRARY OF CONGRESS CATALOGING IN PUBLICATION DATA
Kerouac, Jack, 1922–1969.
Book of blues / Jack Kerouac.
p.   cm.—(Penguin poets)
Contents: San Francisco blues—Richmond Hill blues—Bowery
blues—Macdougal Street blues—Desolation blues—Orizaba 210
blues—Orlanda blues—Cerrada Medellin blues.
ISBN 0 14 05.8700 4
1. Beat generation—Poetry.   I. Title.
PS3521.E735B55   1995
811'.54—dc20   94–45902

Printed in the United States of America
Set in Sabon
Designed by Ann Gold

*This book is dedicated to Philip Whalen
and to the memory of Lew Welch*

CONTENTS

INTRODUCTION

Hard now to go back to the time when Jack Kerouac was writing these poems, the fifties and early sixties, and to the way people then felt poetry *should* be written and what they thought it *should* be saying. Perhaps it hardly matters that much of the poetry of that time found little popular audience, or that it spoke in a way that often confounded its readers. There was a high culture and a low one, and poetry was something significantly attached to the former. The rest was just the passing blur of pop songs and singers, or else the shady edges of black culture and its curiously enduring jazz. Great composers like Stravinsky might use such "forms" for context, and might even get someone like Benny Goodman to play the results. But it always seemed an isolated instance—if not overt slumming.

That was the problem, in fact, not only with music, or poetry, but with writing itself. There was an intense orthodoxy, an insistent critical watchguard, patrolling the borders of legitimate literature to keep all in their necessary places. If one came from habits or ways of speaking or thinking that weren't of the requisite pattern, then the response was abrupt and hostile. Even a poet as Kenneth Rexroth, admitting his complex relation to Kerouac from their times together in San Francisco, wrote of *Mexico City Blues* (1959) that it constituted a "naive effrontery" to have published it as poetry, and that it was "more pitiful than ridiculous." Donald M. Allen's break-through anthology, *The New American Poetry* (1960), soon made clear the resources and authority of what Kerouac and others of his situation were doing, but for a time it seemed that even the viable elders would prove too fixed in their aspirations or disappointments to recognize its authority.

What was the common dream? To be enough of whatever was wanted, to be real, to be included. That meant thinking and talking and moving in one's own legitimacy, one's own given "world," with its persons, habits, humor and place. It was Ginsberg who early on valued particularly Kerouac's crucial insight, that one might write in the same words and manner that one would use in talking to a friend. There didn't have to be a rhetorical "heightening," or a remove from the common, the intimate, and the personal.

Kerouac's friends were then specifically the poets: Allen Ginsberg, Gregory Corso, Philip Lamantia, Gary Snyder, Philip Whalen, Lawrence Ferlinghetti, Michael McClure, Bob Kaufman, Diane di Prima, Lew Welch, Amiri Baraka—and so on through a list now familiar indeed. In contrast, only the novelists John Clellon Holmes and William Burroughs (a source and company for all that "Beat" defined) were in any sense so alert and securing in their relations to him. His sister Caroline ("Nin") and his mother were otherwise safe havens, and he left and returned to their company again and again. Two of the sequences here, "Richmond Hill Blues" (1953) and "Orlanda Blues" (1958), were written while living in his mother's house. The fact of all these relations sounds persistently throughout his writing, and in the poems it is especially emphatic. "Eleven Verses of Garver," (in the section "Orizaba 210 Blues") is literally that, the stories of his friend Bill Garver, described by Kerouac's perceptive biographer Tom Clark (*Jack Kerouac*, 1984) as "a garrulous, aging junkie who occupied the ground-floor apartment" at Orizaba 210, Mexico City, while Kerouac lived in the "mud block" (his words) on the roof. Clark notes it is in this circumstance that Kerouac works as well on *Mexico City Blues* and begins the novel of his "chaste, desperate courtship" of Bill Garver's connection for morphine, *Tristessa* (1960).

All such detail has been usefully spelled out in the various accounts of Kerouac's life. His own sense of what he was doing, either with prose or poems, is equally to the point. In his "Statement on Poetics" for *The New American Poetry* he writes: "Add alluvials to the end of your line when all is exhausted but something has to be said for some specified irrational reason, since reason can never win out, because poetry is NOT a science. The rhythm of how you 'rush' yr statement determines the rhythm of the poem, whether it is a poem in verse-separated lines, or an endless one-line poem called prose . . ." Of course, the parallel is clearly jazz. Thus Edward Foster in his useful work, *Understanding the Beats* (1992), emphasizes Kerouac's own proposal of the relation as follows:

> In a note at the beginning of [*Mexico City Blues*], Ker-ouac says that he wants "to be considered as a jazz poet blowing a long blues in an afternoon jazz session on Sunday," and the individual poems depend, like jazz pieces, on spontaneity and inspiration. Each of the 242 "choruses" is limited by the size of the notebook pages on which he wrote; if an idea (or riff) was not ex-hausted in that space, he would pick it up in the next poem . . .
>
> Most of the choruses are playful and light, and seem-ingly anything that fits the general drift of the rhythm, music, and tone can be added, no matter how incon-gruous it may seem: the sound of a bus outside the building ("Z a r o o o m o o o") an idea for Buddhist lipstick ("Nirvana–No"), nonsense language ("I'm a Agloon") . . . In any case, the poem expresses the poet's sensibility at the moment of writing, and the final poem [of *Mexico City Blues*] identifies "the sound in your mind" as an origin for song . . .

A complaint commonly lodged against Kerouac is that he was at best a self-taught "natural," at worst an example of the *cul de sac* the autodidact in the arts invariably comes to, a solipsistic "world" of his own limitations and confusions.

Blake, naked in his garden, was thus vulnerable. Céline, with his obsessive determination to outplot plot, was also a fool of such kind, as are all heroes of transformation and risk— Henry Miller, D. H. Lawrence and W.C. Williams among them. Otherwise it would be simply "minds like beds, always made up," as Williams said, an enclosure of all that might have been made articulate, felt, tasted, witnessed, and confessed as actual to one's own life, for better or for worse, at last.

But Kerouac was never simply an isolated writer in a time of classic authority and stylistic composure. If one considers Saul Bellow's *The Adventures of Augie March* (1953) in relation to *On the Road* (1957), one will understand precisely what William Burroughs means in saying of Kerouac:

> Kerouac was a writer. That is, he wrote. Many people who call themselves writers and have their names on books are not writers and they can't write—the difference being a bullfighter who fights a bull is different from the bullshitter who makes passes with no bull there. The writer has been *there* or he can't write about it. . . . Sometimes, as in the case of Fitzgerald and Kerouac, the effect produced by a writer is immediate, as if a generation were waiting to be written.

These poems provide an intensely vivid witness of both writer and time. Much is painful, even at times contemptible—the often violent disposition toward women, the sodden celebrations of drink—but it is nonetheless fact of a world still very much our own. Kerouac speaks its painful content, which is not to exempt him from a responsibility therefore. But a world is never simply a choice but a given, and it was not his intent to be brutal if that seems the point. Provincial, yet capable of effecting a common bond, of feeling a joy he could instantly make real for others, he lived in his world as particularly as anyone ever could. What holds it finally all together are *words*, one after another, as he plays, moves, with their sound, follows their lead, shifting from English to Franco-American *joual*, nonsense to sense, reflection to immediate sight and intimate record. He spoke no English until he was five. He wrote incessantly, carrying usually a small spiral notebook in his back pocket so as to "sketch" what occurred on the spot. He was in that old way "serious." He really believed in words.

So one will read here his various recording, invention, improvisation, story. Yet all will be mistaken, misunderstood, if there is not the recognition that this remarkable person is living here, is actual in all that is written. Another poet, Alice Notley, wrote some years after Jack Kerouac's death in 1969 a poem of singular power, "Jack Would Speak through the Imperfect Medium of Alice." This is its close:

> . . . The words are all only one word the perfect
> word—
> My body my alcohol my pain my death are only
> the perfect word as I
> Tell it to you, poor sweet categorizers
> Listen
> Every me I was & wrote
> were only & all (gently)
> That one perfect word

—Robert Creeley
Buffalo, N.Y.

In my system, the form of blues choruses is limited by the small page of the breastpocket notebook in which they are written, like the form of a set number of bars in a jazz blues chorus, and so sometimes the word-meaning can carry from one chorus into another, or not, just like the phrase-meaning can carry harmonically from one chorus to the other, or not, in jazz, so that, in these blues as in jazz, the form is determined by time, and by the musician's spontaneous phrasing & harmonizing with the beat of the time as it waves & waves on by in measured choruses.

It's all gotta be non stop ad libbing within each chorus, or the gig is shot.

—Jack Kerouac

SAN FRANCISCO BLUES

1ST CHORUS

I see the backs
Of old Men rolling
Slowly into black
Stores.

2ND CHORUS

Line faced mustached
Black men with turned back
Army weathered brownhats
Stomp on by with bags
Of burlap & rue
Talking to secret
Companions with long hair
In the sidewalk
On 3rd Street
San Francisco
With the rain of exhaust
   Plicking in the mist
   You see in black
   Store doors—
   Petting trucks farting—
   Vastly city.

3RD CHORUS

3rd St Market to Lease
Has a washed down tile
Tile entrance once white
  Now caked with gum
Of a thousand hundred feet
Feet of passers who
  Did not go straight on
Bending to flap the time
Pap page on back
With smoke emanating
From their noses
But slowly like old
  Lantern jawed junkmen
  Hurrying with the lump
  Wondrous potato bag
    To the avenues of sunshine
    Came, bending to spit,
  & Shuffled awhile there.

4TH CHORUS

The rooftop of the beatup
  tenement
    On 3rd & Harrison
    Has Belfast painted
    Black on yellow
      On the side
    the old Frisco wood is
      shown with weatherbeaten
    rainboards & a
    washed out blue bottle
  once painted for wild
      commercial reasons by
      an excited seltzerite
        as firemen came last
    afternoon & raised the
    ladder to a fruitless
      fire that was not there,
      so, is Belfast singin
          in this time

5TH CHORUS

when brand's forgotten
  taste washed in
  rain the gullies broadened
  & every body gone
the acrobats of the
  tenement
   who dug bel fast
   divers all
   and the divers all dove

  ah
   little girls make
   shadows on the
   sidewalk shorter
  than the shadow
   of death
     in this town—

6TH CHORUS

Fat girls
In red coats
With flap white out shoes

  Monstrous soldiers
  Stalk at dawn
Looking for whores
  And burning to eat up

Harried Mexican Laborers
  Become respectable
  In San Francisco
Carrying newspapers
Of culture burden
And packages of need
Walk sadly reluctant
  To work in dawn
Stalking with not cat
In the feel of their stride
  Touching to hide the sidewalk,
  Blackshiny lastnight parlor
  Shoes hitting the slippery
With hard slicky heels
  To slide & Fall:
      Breboac! Karrak!

7TH CHORUS

Dumb kids with thick lips
And black skin
Carry paper bags
Meaninglessly:
"Stop bothering the cat!"
His mother yelled at him
Yesterday and now
He goes to work
Down Third Street
In the milky dawn
Piano rolling over the hill
To the tune of the English
Fifers in some whiter mine,
'Brick a brack,
 Pliers on your back;
 Mick mack
 Kidneys in your back;
   Bald Boo!
 Oranges and you!
   Lick lock
   The redfaced cock'

8TH CHORUS

Oi yal!
She yawns to lall
   La la—
   Me Loom—
      The weary gray hat
      Peacoat ex sailor
      Marining meekly
      Hands a poop a pocket
      Face
      Lips
Oh   Mo   Sea!
   The long fat yellow
   Eternity cream
   Of the Third St Bus
   Roof swimming like
   A monosyllable
   Armored Mososaur
   Swimming in my Primordial
   Windowpane
      Of pain

9TH CHORUS

Alas! Youth is worried,
Pa's astray.
What so say
  To well dressed ambassadors
  From death's truth
  Pimplike, rich,
  In the morning slick;
  Or sad white caps
  Of snowy sea men
  In San Francisco
Gray streets
  Arm waving to walk
  The Harrison cross
    And earn later sunset
    purple

10TH CHORUS

   Dig the sad old bum
No money
  Presuming to hit the store
And buy his cube of oleo
  For 8 cents
  So in cheap rooms
  At A M   3 30
  He can cough & groan
  In a white tile sink
   By his bed
  Which is used
  To run water in
  And stagger to
  In the reel of wake up
  Middle of the night
    Flophouse Nightmares—
    His death no blackern
    Mine, his Toast's
    Just as well buttered
    And on the one side.

11TH CHORUS

There's no telling
What's on the mind
Of the bony
Character in plaid
Workcoat & glasses
Carrying lunch
Stalking & bouncing
Slowly to his job

Or the beauteous Indian
Girl hurrying stately
Into Marathon Grocery
Run by Greeks
To buy bananas
For her love night,
What's she thinking?
Her lips are like cherries,
Her cheeks just purse them out
All the more to kiss them
And suck their juices out.

12TH CHORUS

A young woman flees an old man,
Mohammedan Prophecy:
And she got avocados
Anyhow.

  The furtive whore
  Looks over her shoulder
While unlocking the door
   Of the tenement
   Of her pimp
Who with big Negro Arkansas
Or East Texas Oilfields
Harry Truman hat's
  Been standin on the street
   All day
    Waiting for the cold girl
    Bending in thincoat in the wind
    And Sunday afternoon drizzle
    To step on it & get some bread
      For Papa's gotta sleep tonite
      And the Chinaman's coming back

13TH CHORUS

"No hunger & no wittles
neither deary"
Said the crone
To Edwin Drood

Okay.
There'll be an answer.
Forthcoming
When the morning wind
Ceases shaking
The man's collar
When there's no starch in't
And Acme Beer
Runs flowing
Into dry gray hats.
When
Dearie
The pennies in the
palm multiply
as you watch

14TH CHORUS

When whistlers stop scowling
Smokers stop sighing
Watchers stop looking
And women stop walking

When gray beards
Grow no more
And pain dont
Take you by surprise
  And bedposts creak
  In rhythm not at morn
  And dry men's bones
  Are not pushed
  By angry meaning pelvic
    Propelled legs of reason
    To a place you hate,
    Then I'll go lay my crown
Body on the heads of 3 men
    Hurrying & laughing
      In the wrong direction,
            my Idol

15TH CHORUS

Sex is an automaton
Sounding like a machine
Thru the stopped up keyhole
—Young men go fastern
    Old men
    Old men are passionately
        breathless
    Young men breathe inwardly
    Young women & old women
    Wait

There was a sound of slapping
When the angel stole come
And the angel that had lost
    Lay back satisfied

Hungry addled red face
With tight clutch
    Traditional Time
    Brief case in his paw
Prowls placking the pavement
    To his office girl's
        Rumped skirt at 5's
            Five O Clock Shadows

16TH CHORUS

Angrily I must insist—
The phoney Negro
Sea captain
With the battered coat
Who looks like
Charley Chaplin in a
movie about now filmed
 in the air by crews
 of raving rabid
 angels drooling happi
 ly
   among the funny fat
   Cherubim
Leading that serious
 Hardjawed sincere
 Negro stud
 In at morn
 For a round of crimes
 Is Lucifer the Fraud

17TH CHORUS

Little girls worry too much
For no one will hurt them
Except the beast
Whom they'd knife
In another life
In the as well East
As West of Bethlehem
And do of it much

  Rhetorical Third Street
Grasping at racket
  Groans & stinky
    I've no time
    To dally hassel
    In your heart's house,
    It's too gray
    I'm too cold—
    I wanta go to Golden,
      That's my home.

18TH CHORUS

  I came a wearyin
  From eastern hills;
Yonder Nabathacaque recessit
The eastward to Aurora rolls,
Somewhere West of Idalia
Or east of Klamath Falls,
One—Lost a blackhaired
  Woman with thin feet
  And red bag hangin
  Who usta walk
    Down Arapahoe Street
  In Denver
   And made all the
    cabbies cry
  And drugstore ponies
  Eating pool in Remsac's
  Sob, to See so Lovely
  All the Time
    And all so Tight
    And young.

19TH CHORUS

Pshaw! Paw's Ford
Got Lost in the Depression
He driv over the Divide
   And forgot to cleave the road
Instead put atomic energy
 In the ass of his machine
And flew to find
  The gory clouds
Of rocky torment
   Far away
   And they fished him
   Outa Miner's Creek
   More dead n Henry
   And a whole lot fonder,
   Podner—
      Clack of the wheel's
      My freight train blues

Third Street I seed

20TH CHORUS

And knowed
  And under ramps I writ
    The poems of the punk
  Who met the Fagin
    Who told him 'Punk
When walkin with me
  To roll a Sleepin drunk
Dont wish ya was back
  Home in yr mother's parlor
  And when the cops
    Come ablastin
  With loaded 45's
    Dont ask for gold
Or silver from my purse,
  Its milken hassel
  Will be strewn
    And scattered
    In the sand
    By an old bean can
      And dried up kegs
      We'd a sat & jawed on—

21ST CHORUS

Roll my bones
In the Mortiary
 My terms
    And deeds of mortgagry
 And death & taxes
   All wrapt up.'

Little anger Japan
  Strides holding bombs
To blow the West
 To Fuyukama's
Shrouded Mountain Top
 So the Lotus Bubble
Blossoms in Buddha's
 Temple Dharma Eye
May unfold from
   Pacific Center
   Inward Out & Over
    The Essence Center World

22ND CHORUS

For the world's an Eye
And the universe is Seeing
Liquid
Rare
Radiant.

Eccentrics from out of town
　Better not fill in
　　This blank
　For a job on my gray boat
　And Monkeysuits I furnish.

　Batteries of ad men
　Marching arm in arm
　　Thru the pages
　　Of Time & Life

23RD CHORUS

The halls of M C A

Singing Deans
In the college morning
Preferable to dry cereal
When no corn mush

Cops & triggers
Magazine pricks
  Dastardly Shadows
And Phantom Hero ines.

Swing yr umbrella
 At the sidewalk
 As you pass
 Or tap a boy
   On the shoulder
   Saying "I say
   Where is Threadneedle
                    Street?"

24TH CHORUS

San Francisco is too sad
Time, I cant understand
Fog, shrouds the hills in
Makes unshod feet so cold
Fills black rooms with day
  Dayblack in the white windows
  And gloom in the pain of pianos:
Shadows in the jazz age
  Filing by; ladders of flappers
  Painters' white bucket
  Funny 3 Stooge Comedies
    And fuzzy headed Hero
    Moofle Lip suckt it all up
    And wondered why
    The milk & cream of heaven
      Was writ in gold leaf
      On a book—big eyes
      For the world
        The better to see—

25TH CHORUS

And big lips for the word
And Buddhahood
And death.
   Touch the cup to these sad lips
Let the purple grape foam
In my gullet deep
 Spread saccharine
   And crimson carnadine
   In my vine of veins
 And shoot power
   To my hand
     Belly heart & head—
       This Magic Carpet
       Arabian World
       Will take us
         Easeful Zinging
       Cross the Sky
       Singing Madrigals

26TH CHORUS

To horizons of golden
Moment emptiness
Whither whence uncaring
Dizzy ride in space
To red fires
Beyond the pale,
Rosy gory outlooks
Everywhere.

San Francisco is too old
Her chimnies lean
And look sooty
After all this time
Of waiting for something
To happen
Betwixt hill & house—
Heart & heaven.

27TH CHORUS

San Francisco
San Francisco
You're a muttering bum
  In a brown beat suit
  Cant make a woman
  On a rainy corner

Your corners open out
San Francisco
To arc racks
Of the Seals
  Lost in vapors
  Cold and bleak.

28TH CHORUS

You're as useless
As a soda truck
Parked in the rain
With cases of pretty red
   Orange green & Coca Cola
    Brown receiving rain
   Drops like the sea
    Receiveth driving spikes
Welling in the navel void.

I also have loud poems:
Broken plastic coverlets
  Flapping in the rain
   To cover newspapers
   All printed up
    And plain.

29TH CHORUS

Guys with big pockets
In heavy topcoats
And slit scar
Head bands down
The middle of their hair
All Bruce Barton combed
Stand surveying Harrison
Folsom & the Ramp
And the redbrick clock
Wishin they had a woman
Or some money, honey

Westinghouse Elevators
Are full of pretty girls
With classy cans
And cute pans
And long slim legs
And eyes for the boss
At quarter of four.

30TH CHORUS

Old Age is an Indian
With gray hair
And a cane
In an old coat
 Tapping along
 The rainy street
  To see the pretty oranges
 And the stores
   On his big day
When the dog's let out.

Somewhere in this snow
I see little children raped
By maniacal sex fiends
Eager to make a break
But the F B I
In the form of Ted
 Stands waiting
  Hand on gun
 In the Paranoiac
  Summer time
  To come.

31ST CHORUS

I knew an angel
 In Mexico City
Call'd La Negra
Who the Same eyes
  Had as Sebastian
  And was reincarnated
    To suffer in the poker
    House rain
    Who had the same eyes
      As Sebastian
    When his Nirvana came

Sambati was his name.

Must have had one leg once
And expensive armpit canes
  And traveled in this rain
  With youthful hidden pain

32ND CHORUS

Beautiful girls
  Just primp
    But beautiful boys
    Do suffer.

White wash rain stain
Gravel roof glass black
  Red wood blue neon
  Green elevators
  Birds that change color
  And white ants
    Climbing to your knee
      Earnest for deliverance.

33RD CHORUS

It was a mournful day
The B O Bay was gray
Old man angry-necks
Stomped to escape sex
And find his Television
In the uptown vision
 Of the milk & secret
   Blossom curtain
   Creak it.

Cheese it the cops!
Ram down the lamb!
 700 Camels
 In Pakistan!

Milk will curdle, honey,
If you sit on stony penises
Three times moving up & down
And 7 times around

34TH CHORUS

While young boys peek
  In the Hindu temple window
   To grow
     And come
   To A-mer-ri-kay
     And be long silent types
     In the night clerk cage
   Waiting for railroad calls
     And hints from Pakistan
     Beluchistan and Mien Mo
     That Mahatmas
     Havent left the field
       And tinkle bells
       And cobra flutes
       Still haunt our campfires
     In the calm & peaceful
       Night—
         Stars of India

35TH CHORUS

And speak bashfully
  Thru strong brown eyes
  Of olden strengths
    And bad boy episodes
    And a father
      With sacred cows
    A wandering in his field.
    "Rain on, O cloud!"

    The taste of worms
    Is soft & salty
    Like the sea,
    Or tears.

    And raindrops
    That dont know
  You've been deceived
  Slide on iron
    Raggedly gloomy

36TH CHORUS

Falling off in wind.

I got the San Francisco
      blues
Bluer than misery
I got the San Francisco blues
Bluer than Eternity
      I gotta go on home
      Fine me
      Another
      Sanity

I got the San Francisco
      blues
Bluer than heaven's gate,
      mate,
   I got the San Francisco blues
Bluer than blue paint,
      Saint,—
      I better move on home
      Sleep in
      My golden
      Dream again

37TH CHORUS

I got the San Acisca blues
Singin in the street all day
    I got
    The San Acisca
    Blues
Wailin in the street all day
    I better move on, podner,
    Make my West
    The Eastern Way—

San
  Fran
Cis
   Co—
San
  Fran
Cis
   Co
     Oh—
        ba
         by

38TH CHORUS

Ever see a tired
    ba by
Cryin to sleep
    in its mother's arms
Wailin all night long
     while the locomotive
Wails on back
A cry for a cry
In the smoke and the lamp
Of the hard ass night

  That's how I
     fee-
        eel—
    That's how
       I fee-eel!
  That's *how*
         I feel—
What a deal!
Yes I'm goin ho
         o
          ome

39TH CHORUS

Yes I'm goin
on
home
today

Tonight I'll be ridin
The 80 mile Zipper
And flyin down the Coast
Wrapt in a blanket

Cryin
And cold

So brother
Pour me a drink
  I got lots of friends
  From coast to coast
  And ocean to ocean
      girls
    But when I see
    A bottle a wine
    And see that it's full
    I like to open it
      And take of it my fill

40TH CHORUS

And when my head gets dizzy
And friends all laugh
And money pours
    from my pocket
And gold from my ears
And silver flies out
    and rubies explode
I'll up & eat
And sing another song
And drop another grape
  In my belly down

Cause you know
What Omar Khayyam said
  Better be happy
  With the happy grape
  As make long faces
    And groan all night
     In search of fruit
      That dont exist

41ST CHORUS

So Mister Engineer
And Mister Hoghead
  Conductor Jones
And you head brakeman
  And you, tagman
        on this run
  Give me a hiball
Boomer's or any kind
  Start that Diesel
  All 3 Units
    Less roll on down that rail
    See Kansas City by dawn
    Or grass of Amarilla
Or rooftops of Old New York
  Or banksides green with grass
    In April
      Anywhere

42ND CHORUS

I'd better be a poet
Or lay down dead.

Little boys are angels
Crying in the street
Wear funny hats
Wait for green lights
  Carry bust out tubes
    Around their necks
    And roam the railyards
    Of the great cities
     Looking for locomotives
  Full of shit
    Run down to the waterfront
    And dream of Cathay
    Hook spars with Gulls
     Of athavoid thought.

43RD CHORUS

Little Cody Deaver
A San Francisco boy
  Hung by hair of heroes
Growing green & thin
  And soft as sin
  From the tie piles
Of the railer road
  Track where Tokay
  Bottles rust in dust
  Waiting for the term
  Of partiality
  To end up there
    In heaven high
    So's loco can
    Come home
    Con poco coco.

44TH CHORUS

Little heroes of the dead
Found a nickle instead
And bought a Borden half & half
  Orange Sherbert & vanil milk
    Trod the pavements
    Of unfall Frisco
    Waiting for its earthquake
  To waver houses men
    And streets to spindle
    Drift to fall at Third
    Street Number 6–15
Where Bank now stands
Jack London was born
And saw gray rigging
At the 'barcadero
  Pier, His bier
  commemorated in marble
  To advertise the stone
    Of vaults where money rots.

45TH CHORUS

Inquisitive plaidshirt
Pops look at trucks
In the afternoon
While Mulligan's
Stewing on the stove
And Calico spreads
  Her milk & creamy legs
  For advertising salesman
    Passing thru from Largo
  Oregon where water
      Runs the Willamette down
      By blasted to-the-North
        Volcanic ashes seft.

46TH CHORUS

Babies born screaming
   in this town
Are miserable examples
   of what happens
Everywhere.

 Bein Crazy is
 The least of my worries.

Now the sun's goin down
In old San Fran
 The hills are in a haze
 Of Shroudy afternoon—
 Bent withered Burroughsian
 Greeks pass
   In gray felt hats
   Expensively pearly
   On bony suffer heads

47TH CHORUS

And old Indian bo's
With no stockings on
Just Chinese Shuffle
Opium shoes
Take the snaily constitutional
Down 3rd St gray & lost
& Hard to see.

Tragic burpers
With scars of snow
Bound bigly
Huge to find it
To the train
Of time & pain
Waiting at the terminal.

Young punk mankind
Three abreast
Go thriving downwards
In the hellish street.

48TH CHORUS

Red shoes of the limpin whore
Who drags her blues
  From shore to shore
    Along the stores
    Lookin for a millioinaire
      For her time's up
      And she got no guts
      And the man aint comin
      And I'm no where.

He aint done nothin
  But change hats
And go to work
And light a new cigar
  And stands in doorway
Swingin the 8 inch
Stogie all around
  Arc ing to see
Mankind's vast

49TH CHORUS

Sea restless crown
Come rolling bit by bit
  From offices of gloom
  To homes of mortuary
  Hidden Television
  Behind the horse's
   Clock in Hopalong
   The Burper's bestfriend
    Ten gat waving
    Far from children
    Sadly waving
    From the balcony
    Above this street
  Where Acme Paper
      Torn & Tattered
  S'down the parade
  Thrown to clebrate
  McParity's return:

50TH CHORUS

All ties in
Like anacin.

Well
    So unlock the door
    And go to supper
And let the women cook it,
  Light's on the hill
  The guitar's a-started
    Playing by itself
    The shower of heaven notes
    Plucked by a gypsy woman
    In some old dream
    Will bless it all
      I see furling out
      Below—

51ST CHORUS

The laundress has bangs
  And pursy lips
  And thin hips
  And sexy walk
And goes much faster
  When she knows
    The booty in her
      laundry bag
    Is undiscovered
      And unknown
      And so no cops watching
              she steps on it
              t'escape the Feds
              of Wannadelancipit
              Here in the Standard
                  Building
              Flying High
                  the
              Riding Horse
        A Red—

52ND CHORUS

None of this means
anything
  For krissakes speak up
        & be true
    Or shut up
    & Go to bed

Dead

  The wash is waving goodbye
  Towards Oakland's russet

I know there are huge clouds
Ballooning beyond the bay

  And out Potato Patch,
  The snowy sea away,
  The milk is furling
    Huge and roly
      Poly burly puffy

53RD CHORUS

Pulsing push
To come on in
Inundate Frisco
 Fill the rills
And ride the ravines
And sneak on in
With Whippoorwill
   To-hoo— To-wa!
      The Chinese call it woo
      The French les brumes
      The British
            Fog
L A
   Smog
Heaven
      Cellar door

54TH CHORUS

Communities of houses
Caparisoned by sunlight
On the last & fading hill
Of America a-rollin
    Rollin
To the Western Chill

And delicacies of statues
Hewn by working men
Neoned, tacked on,
Pressed against the sign
    Mincin
    Mincin
To sell the swellest coupon

Understand?

Light on the fronts
    of old buildings
Like in New York
In December dusks
When hats point to sea

55TH CHORUS

This means
    that everything
       has some home
       to come to
Light has windows
    balconies of iron
       like New Orleans

It also has all space
 And I have windows
    balconies of iron
        like New Orleans

I also have all space

And St Louis too

  Light follows rivers
   I do too

  Light fades, I pass

56TH CHORUS

Light illuminates
  The intense cough
Of young girls in love
Hurrying to sell their
    future husband
On the Market St
    Parade

Light makes his face
    reddern
 Her white mask

She sucks to bone him dry
 And make him happy
 Make him cry
  Make him baby
 Stay by me.

57TH CHORUS

Crooks of Montreal
  Tossing up their lighters
    To a cigarette of snow
    Intending to plot evil
    And break the pool machine
      Tonight off Toohey's head
      And the Frisco fire team
      Come howling round
      The corner of the dream

58TH CHORUS

Immense the rivets
In the broadsides
Of battleships
   Fired upon head on
   In face to face combat
   In the Philippines
    Anchored Alameda
    Overtime for toilets
     On Labor Day

59TH CHORUS

IL
W
U
  Has tough white seamen
  Scrapping snow white hats
  In favor of iron clubs
  To wave in inky newsreels
  When Frisco was a drizzle
      And Curran all sincere,
        Bryson just a baby,
  Reuther bloodied up,
  —When publications
Of Union pamphleteers
  Featured human rock jaws
  Jutting Editorialese
  Composed by angry funny
      redhead editors
  Walking with their heads down
    To catch the evening fleet
      And wave goodbye to sailors
      passing rosely dreams
      Into a sparkling cannon
      Gray & spicked & span
        To shine the Admiral
        In his South Pacific pan—

60TH CHORUS

No such luck
  For Potter McMuck
Who broke his fist
On angry mitts
In fist fights
Falling everywhere
From down Commercial
  To odd or even
All the piers
  Blang! Bang!
  I L W U had a hard time
  And so did N A M
  And S P A M
  And as did A M

61ST CHORUS

YOU INULT ME EVERY NIME, MALN BWANO
Ladies and Gentle-man
  The phoney woiker
  You here see
    Got can one time
  In Toonisfreu
   Ger ma nyeee
  Becau he had
       no dime
To give the con duck teur
   Yo see he stiffled
     For his miffle
And couldnt cough a little
   Bill de juice ran
       down his Sfam.

62ND CHORUS

JULIEN LOVE'S SOUND
"All
    right!
Here we are
  with all the little lambs.
Has anyone disposed
  of my old man
Last night?
    Mortuary deeds,
    Dead,
  Drink, me down
  Table or two,
  Wher'd you put it
     Kerouac?
  The bottoms in your bag
 Of cellar heaven doors
And hellish consistencies
  Gelatinous & composed
  Will bang & break
Apon the time clock
  Beat prow stone bong
  Boy
  Before I give YOU
  An idgit of the
   Kind Love Legend"

63RD CHORUS

JULIEN LOVE'S JUDGMENT
"Seriously boy
  This San Francisco
      Blues of yours
  Like shark fins
      the summer before
  And was it Sarie
  Sauter Finnegan
    Some gal before—
    It's a farce
      For funny you
                you know?
  I dont think I'll buy it"

  Slit in the ear
    By a bolo knife
  Savannah Kid just nodded
  At the beast that
    Hides.

  Secret
  Poetry
  Deceives
Simply

64TH CHORUS

California evening is like Mexico
The windows get golden oranges
The tattered awnings flap
Like dresses of old Perdido
  Great Peruvian Princesses
    In the form of Negro Whores
    Go parading down the sidewalk
    Wearing earrings, sweet perfume
      Old Weazel Warret

    tradesmen
     sick of selling
     out their stores stand in
        the evening lineup
        before identifying cops
        they cannot understand
        in the clouds of can
         and iron moosing
         marshly morse
         of over head

65TH CHORUS

Daughters of Jerusalem
Prowling like angry felines
Statuesque & youthful
 From the well
 Embarrassed but implacable
 And watched by hungry worriers
  Filling out the whitewall
    Car with 1000 pounds
    Of "Annergy!
     Thats what I got!
    An-nergy!"
   To burn up Popocatepetl's
   Torch of ecstasy.

The neons redly twangle
 Twinkle cute & clean
 Like Millbrae cherry
  Nipptious tostle
   Flowers tattled
   Petal for the joss stick
   Stuck in neon twaddles
   To advertise a bar
 —All over SanFranPisco
 The better is the pain

66TH CHORUS

—"Switch to Calvert"
  Runs an arrow eating
    Bulb by bulb
    Across the bulbous
        Whisky bottle
And under the Calvert clock

  Tastes better!   Everyone
        Tastes better
        All the time

  And fieldhands
  That aint got aznos
    But the same south Mexican
    Evening soft shoe
        walk
  Slow in dusts of soft
  in Ac to pan
  Here in Frisco City
        American
   The same way walk
     To buy some vegetables

67TH CHORUS

For the bedsprings on the roof
  Not keep the rain on out
Or bombed out huts
  In dumpland—Blue
Workjacket, shino pants,
   It's like Mexico all violet
    At ruby rose & velvet
     Sun on down
      On down
    Sun on down
     Sundown

Red blood bon neon
  Bon runs   don   blon

By Barrett
      Wimpole
          Trackmeet

68TH CHORUS

And like Mexico the deep
Gigantic scorpic haze
Of shady curtain night
  Bein drawn on civilized
  And Fellaheen will howl
  Where the cows of mush
Rush to hide their sad
  Tan hides in the stonecrump
  Mumps bump top of hill
    Out Mission Way
    Holy Cows of Cross
    And Lick Monastery

          Velvet for our meat
          Hamburgers

And doom of pained nuns
  Or painted
          One
  Mexico is like Universe

69TH CHORUS

And Third Street a Sun
Showing just how's done
The light the life the action
The limp of worried reachers
Crawling up the Cuba street
In almost dark
To find the soften bell
Creaming Meek on corner
One by one, Tem, Tim,
Click, gra, rattapisp,
Ting, Tang—

Blink!   Off
Run!   Arrow!
Cut! Winkle! Twinkle!
Fill
Piss! Pot!
The lights of coldmilk
supper hill streets
make me davenport
and cancel Ship.

70TH CHORUS

  3rd St is like Moody St
Lowell Massachusetts
It has Bagdad blue
  Dusk down sky
  And hills with lights
 And pale the hazel
   Gentle blue in the
        burned windows
Of wooden tenements,
   And lights of bars,
        music brawl,
     "Hoap!" "Hap!" & "Hi"
   In the street of blood
   And bells billygoating
     Boom by at the ache
          of day
   The break of personalities
     Crossing just once
     In the wrong door

71ST CHORUS

Nevermore to remain
  Nevermore to return
  —The same hot hungry
    harried hotel
    wild Charlies dozzling
      to fold the
      Food papers in the
        mahogany talk
  Of television reading room
Balls are walled
  and withered
  and long fergit.

Moody Lowell Third Street
  Sick & tired bedsprings
  Silhouettes of brownlace
    eve night dowse—
All that—
  And outsida town
  The aching snake
  Pronging underground
    To come eat up
    Us the innocent
      And insincere in here

72ND CHORUS

And Budapest Counts
Driving lonely mtn. cars
On the hem of the grade
Of the lip curve hill
Where Rockly meets
  Out Market & More—
  The last shore—
   View of the sea
    Seal

  Only Lowell has for sea
  The imitative Merrimac

  And Frisco has for
    snake
   The crowdy earthquake
    cataract
And Hydrogen Bombs
    of Hope
 Lost in the blue
    Pacific
  Empty sea

73RD CHORUS

Bakeries gladly bright
Filled with dour girls
Buying golden pies
For sullen brooding boys

On 3rd St in the night

But by day
  The Greek Armenian
    Milk of honey
  Bee baclava maker
  Puts his sugars
  On the counter
    For bums with avid jaws
  And hollow eyes
    Eager to eat
    Their last dainty.

74TH CHORUS

Marchesa Casati
Is a living doll
Pinned on my Frisco
Skid row wall

Her eyes are vast
Her skin is shiny
    Blue veins
And wild red hair
Shoulders sweet & tiny

Love her
Love her
        Sings the sea
    Bluely
  Moaning
In the Augustus John
        de John
            back ground.

75TH CHORUS

Her eyes are living dangers
'll Leap you
From a page
Wearing the same insanity
  The sweet unconcernedly
  Italian humanity
    Glaring from black eyebrows
      To ask
      Of Renaissance:
    "What have you done now
    After 3 hundred years
    But create the glary witness
    Which out this window
    Shows a pale green
      Friscan hill
      The last green hill
      Of America
        With a cut   a band

76TH CHORUS

Of brown red road
  Coint round
  By architects of hiways
    To show the view
      To ledge travellers
  Of Frisco, City, Bay
    And Sea
      As all you do is drive around
  —By Groves of lonesome
    Redwood trees
    Isolated
    In physical isolation
    On the bare lump
    Hill like people
      Of this country
    Who walk alone
      In streets all day
      Forbidden
      To contact physically
        Anybody
        So desirable—

77TH CHORUS

They kill'd all painters
Drown'd—Made wash
The smothering crone
Of Cathay,
  Flower of Malaya,
  And Dharma saws,
  Gat it all in,
    Like wash,
    Call'd it Renascence
    And then wearied
      From the globe—
      Hill, last hill
      Of Western World
        Is cut around
        Like half attempted
        Half castrated
        Protrudient breast
         Of milk
        From wild staring earth

78TH CHORUS

—The last scar
America was able
  To create
  The uttermost hill
  Beyond which is just
       Pacific
  And no more sc-cuts
  And Alamos neither
  But that can be rolled
  In satisfying sea
  Absolved of suicide—
    Except that now
    They're blasting fishermen
     Apart?"

79TH CHORUS

"Beyond that fruitless sea"
—So speaks Marchesa
Mourning the Renaissance
And still the breeze
Is sweet & soft
 And cool as breasts
 And wild as sweet dark eyes.

Sits in her spirit
Like she wont be long
And bright about it
 All the time, like short
    star

    An angry proud beauty
    Of Italy

80TH CHORUS

San Francisco Blues
Written in a rocking chair
  In the Cameo Hotel
  San Francisco Skid row
  Nineteen Fifty Four.

This pretty white city
On the other side of the country
  Will no longer be
  Available to me
  I saw heaven move
  Said "This is the End"
  Because I was tired
  of all that portend.

  And any time you need
        me
Call
    I'll be at the other
       end
  Waiting
        at the final hall

RICHMOND HILL BLUES

DULUOZ
Name derived from early
    morning sources
In a newspaper office
Long Ago in Lowell Mass
When birds were shitting
On the canal
And Sperm was Floating
    among the Redbrick Walls
Of a Morn that had Smoke
Pouring from a Christian Hill
    Chimney—
Ah Sire, Duluoz,
  King of my Thoughts,
    Salute!
(Kick another can of beer)

THAT'S WHAT I SAID
Not what I thot I meant
O Sin-of-a-Bitch
But what I out loud said
Not—again—what in
    retrospect
And banalizing sedeora ing
    of my garage
Made it
Say what you mean
  A poem is a lark
  A pie

SCHLITZ (A drunken vision of a can of beer)
Beaded melt hotwave waters
Of outside hydrated juices
Flowing down Made in USA
& Brooklyn New York
Genuine, holed triangular.

WIFE & 3
Little Cathy gladdy
  with sun cheeks
   beeted
Jamie hiding hugging
  her knees
Mother Earwicker solemn,
   lovely, flesh legs
    white
King John Fartitures
  of Hop Top Heap
   Cassadee-ing in
   his Kingdom
Jamie of mother's sweetly
  sweet goodheart breast
Showing oldlady teeth
   of littlegirl glee
 And pudgy arms locked

Tristesse in the little
  hopeless Fingers,
Faisse in the shot,
   the radiant sun,
The shine of San Jose
O
  Grass
       Peotés of time!

  Steps, lost davenports,
   eternities,
Hot Night Birds,
  Billy Holiday!
—Make the quaker
  give his cream

ANY TIME
Any time you want
A write a fucken poem
Ope this book
& Scream no more
But Cream
Cry
Fret not
  Flow
  Flay
  Fray the edge of Froy
Make Frogs Alliterate
    Bekkek! Bekkek!
      Koak! Koak!
      Carra Quax!
      Carra qualquus
          Kerouacainius!

EVEN JOYCE
Even he, Joyce,
    had love—
Even blind poets

AUDEN HAD NO ASS

Auden had no ass
Butler had no balls
Carew had no crash
Dyck had no dick
Egrets had no erse
Fart had no fuck
George had no Gyzm
His honou had no H
I J Fox had no wife
J Fox had no Joke
Kerou had no Ka
Ling Woe had no Rice
M & N had no Moola
    (a lot!)
Novales had no Nodes
O vum had no Ollie
    (O'Neill Mc Shanahan)
P-ew had no Push
Quasi Quean had no Queasy
    feelings
R had no heart
Studentio
    had
        no
            Stok
To
   v
     e
    l
     e
       n
      l
       s

h   had
      no

        T
          u
          p

Uvalde had no Upstarts
Vedichad no Velda
Velda had no Vim

Vish had no Rush
        her
          Vim
                hid
                    his
    Or pit his ass
    gainst my pen

U had no V
V had no Victory
U V W had no
      Pesco
            X no Y or Z

THE POET

So many times since
I've seen the poet
of Greenwich Village
Cutting to work in the gray dawn
With a lunchpail &
   bleak haircut
  Eyes to the Hudson
   Nostril to the street
   To winter, work, beneficence,
Meals, fare of folly
So many times since
I've seen the poet
Who wrote rhythms & rhymes
To be mad in Minetta's
And Minetta Lane
  Go Hurrying to Work
  Sex hung, sexed, psycho-
    analyzed?
To work in the unpoetic dawn

Mornings after I'd got drunk
with Lucien & Allen
  & Allied Angels
In the Vast Manhattan
    Fish—
O America!
  Songs!
  Poems!
   Altos!   Tenors!
      Blow!
(Poet is Dead)

THUNDER

Thunder makes a booming
    noise like windows
  Being hysterically quietly
    closed—
So Papa fell down the stairs
    of time
In spite of holy water
  And all yr mixed drinks
    in
  Eternity

EMILY DICKINSON

Ere so sober Emily
  Did New England sow
  With brooms of activity
  I'd the tree-rock spoken to.
But it only said to me
"This sleet's crack
  You hear cracking my hide
  Is the voice of olden poets
  Not far from rocks of here
  Did their olden eyes
  On nature bestow blue
  —" I said
"Ah Oh How So Sad."

I said—"And graves?"
And I said "Darling
Supposing it should
  To nature
  Suddenly occur
  To make unending poets
  Unendingly Blow"

Nature Said: "Mean,
  I dont know what you
Mean"—
"Ah Nature, Ah Rock,"
I cried, "Nobody's Bone
  Has so suffusèd been,
  No burden of boredom
  Greater
  No love colder
  No love life less
  No grave nearer
  Always
  Than Ye Bard"

ROSE
"Ah Rose," I cried,
"Shine in the Phosphorescent
Night."

BUG
And to the little bug which am myself
            I said
"Bug, lip, tip, tit of time,
 Try, take, take, flake, fly,
 Love is passing yr. cheekbones
 On the phosphorescent transparent
            wing
 Of Kafka's cheese consuming
    Metamorphosed Bug"

HORROR
So then I saw horror,
And I cried,
"Horrer, leave me er lone."
 Horrer-horror laid me bone
 By bone in a bag of dirt,
 I was broiled in the oven
 Of heaven in the silver foil
 Of Devil Jesus God
 Which is Yr Holy Trinity

———

SMILES
Smiles pull flesh from cheek
Over pearls of bone
  And make the watcher see
  The quake of cream
  In eyes of stone

ON TEARS
Tears is the break of my brow,
The moony tempestuous
    sitting down
In dark railyards
When to see my mother's face
Recalling from the waking vision
I wept to understand
The trap mortality
And personal blood of earth
Which saw me in—
  Father father
  Why hast thou forsaken me?
Mortality & unpleasure
Roam this city—
Unhappiness my middle name
  I want to be saved,—
  Sunk—can't be
  Won't be
  Never was made to—
  So retch!

WHEN OLD

When I began to grow old
  And could feel my left arm
     numben
  And brain resisted hope,
  Will sat sleeping
  Energy thubbd exhausted
    in my eye
  And love fled me—
  When the worst news
    Was brought to me
    And I exulted to be alone
   Go die
     I had a vision of
      the saint
     Misunderstood & too tired
      to explain why
     And sweet intentioned
      in another day—
Even Stanley Gould'll
    go to heaven

BOP

Sweet little dop a la pee—
Bit bit piano tip
  tinkle plips
 And smash prop brushes
In the little numb moment
  um

I KNOW
I know that I cannot write
  verse
But this is my beercan short
  line
Book so bear with me
  invisible
Reader and let me goof
  even
When I'm sick & have no
  ideas

GOD
Sitting over our meanings
Egomaniac God,
Lonely slick & rain glint
Also uses irritating us
In the Real.

HOPES
Poetry doesnt know:
The air conditioner
Not in use in winter
Is like my hopes—
Half in, half out,
 Green on a whitewall,
 S'only good to cast
A long shadow
 In the bleak street light

TREE
But a tree has
    a living suffering shape
Is spread in half
   by 2 limbed fate
Rises from gray rain
    pavements
To traffic in the bleak
    brown air
Of cities radar television
    nameless dumb &
    numb mis connicumb
  Throwing twigs the
    color of ink
  To white souled
    heaven, with
  A reality of its own uses

TENORMAN

Sweet sad young tenor
Horn slumped around neck
Bearded full of junk
Slouches waiting
For Apocalypse,
Listens to the new
Negro raw trumpet kid
Tell him the wooden news;
And the beat of the bass
The bass—drives in
Drummer drops a bomb
Piano tinkle tackles
Sweet tenor lifting
All American sorrows
Raises mouthpiece to mouth
And blows to finger
  The iron sounds

BOWERY BLUES

For I
Prophesy
That the night
Will be bright
With the gold
Of old
In the inn
Within.

Cooper Union Cafeteria—late cold March afternoon, the street
(Third Avenue) is cobbled, cold, desolate with trolley tracks—
Some man on the corner is waving his hand down No-ing some-
body emphatically and out of sight behind a black and white pil-
lar, cold clowns in the moment horror of the world—A Porto
Rican kid with a green stick, stooping to bat the sidewalk but
changing his mind and halting on—Two new small trucks
parked—The withery grey rose stone building across the street
with its rime heights in the quiet winter sky, inside are quiet
workers by neon entablatures practicing fanning lessons with the
murderous Marbo—A yakking blonde with awful wide smile is
makking her mouth lip talk to an old Bodhisattva papa on the
sidewalk, the tense quickness of her hard working words—Mean-
while a funny bum with no sense trys to panhandle them and is
waved away stumbling, he doesnt care about society women em-
barrassed with paper bags on sidewalks—Unutterably sad the
broken winter shattered face of a man passing in the bleak ripple
—Followed by a Russian boxer with an expression of Baltic lost-
ness, something grim and Slavic and so helplessly beyond my
conditional ken or ability to evaluate and believe that I shudder
as at the touch of cold stone to think of him, the sickened old
awfulness of it like slats of wood wall in an old brewery truck

Shin Mc Ontario with
no money, no bets, no
health, pauls on by
pawing his inside coat
no hope of ever
seeing Miami again
since he lost his pickles
on Orchard Street
and his father
S t u h t e l f e d e h r e d
him to hospitals
Of gray
bleak
bone
drying
in the moon
that mortifies his coat
and words sing
what mind
brings

Bleeding bloody seamen
Of Indian England
Battering in coats
Of Third Ave noo
With no sense and their brows
Streaked with wine sop
Blood of ogligit
Sad adventurers
Far from the pipe
Of Liverpool
The bean of bone
Bottle Liffey brown
Far   hung   unseen
Top tippers
Of o cean wave.

God bless & sing for them
As I   can not

*

Cooper Union Blues,
The Musak is too Sod.
The gayety of grave
Candidates makes
My gut weep
And my brains
Are awash
Down the side of the
        blue orange table
As little sneery snirfling
Porto Rican hero
Ba t ts by booming
His coat pocket
Fisting to the Vicinity
Where Mortuary
Waits for bait.
(What kind of service
Do broken barrels give?)
   O have pity
      Bodhisattva
      Of Intellectual
      Ra   diance!

Save the world from her eyebrows
Of beautiful illusion
Hope, O hope,
O Nope, O pope

_____

Crowded coat ers
In a front seat

Car, gray & grim,
Push on thru
To the basketball

*

Various absurd parades—
The strict in tact
Intent man with
Broken back
Balling his suitcase
Down from Washington
Building in the night
Passing little scaggly
Childreyn with Ma's
Of mopey hope.

————

Too sad, too sad
The well kept
Clean cut
Ferret man.

*

And the old blue Irishman
With untenable dignity
Beer bellying home
To drowsy dowdy TV
Suppers of gravy
And bile—
Wearing old new coats
Meant to be smooth on youths
Wrinkled on his barrel
Like sea wind
Infatuating sea eyes

To thinkin
Ripples & old age
Are real.

*

Poor young husbandry
  With coat of tan
Digging change in palms
  For bleaker coffees
Than afternoon gloom
  Where work of stone
Was endowed
  With tired hope.
Hope   O hope
Cooper Union Hope
O Bowery of Hopes!
O absence!
O blittering real
Non staring redfaced
Wild reality!
Hiding in the night
Like my dead father
I see the crystal
Shavings shifting
Out of sight
Dropping pigeons of light
To the Turd World
Enought, sad ones—
False petals
Of pure lotus
In drugstore windows
Where cups of O
Are smoked

Paddy Mc Gilligan
Muttering in the street

Just hit town
From C a l c i   bleak

Ole Mop Polock Pat
Angry as a cat
About to stumble
Into the movie
Of the night
Through which he sees
M   oo   da   lands
Un seen
Like waking in the night
To transcendental Milk
In the room

———

Sad Jewish respectable
rag men with trucks
And watchers
Shaking cloth
Into the gutter
Saying   I dunno, no, no,
As gray green hat
Sits on their heads
Protecting them
From Infinity above
Which shines with white
Wide & brown black clouds
As Liberty Sun
Honks over the Sea
Sending Ships
From inner sea
Free
To de rool york
Pock Town of Part
Shelf High Hawk

Man   Dung   Town.
        Rinkidink Charley is Crazy.

                    *

Ugly pig
Burping
In the sidewalk
As surrealistic
   Typewriters
   Swim exploding by
   And bigger marines
   Lizard thru the side
   Of the gloom
   Like water
    For this
is the Sea
Of
Reality.

                *

The story of man
Makes me sick
Inside, outside,
I dont know why
Something so conditional
And all talk
Should hurt me so.

I am hurt
I am scared
I want to live
I want to die
I dont know
Where to turn
In the Void

And when
To cut
Out

———

For no Church told me
No Guru holds me
No advice
Just stone
Of New York
And on the cafeteria
We hear
The saxophone
Of dead Ruby
Died of Shot
In Thirty Two,
Sounding like old times
And de bombed
Empty decapitated
Murder by the clock.
And I see Shadows
Dancing into Doom
In love, holding
Tight the lovely asses
Of the little girls
In love with sex
Showing themselves
In white undergarments
At elevated windows
Hoping for the Worst.

I cant take it
Anymore
If I cant hold
My little behind
To me in my room

Then it's goodbye
Sangsara
For me
Besides
Girls arent as good
As they look
And Samadhi
Is better
Than you think
When it stars in
Hitting your head
In with Buzz
Of glittergold
Heaven's Angels
Wailing
Saying
We ve been waiting for you
  Since Morning, Jack
—Why were you so long
  Dallying in the sooty room?
  This Transcendental Brilliance
  Is the better part
  (Of Nothingness
  I sing)

Okay.
Quit.
Mad.
Stop.

————

MACDOUGAL STREET BLUES

IN THE FORM OF 3 CANTOS

*

CANTO UNO

The goofy foolish
    human parade
Passing on Sunday
    art streets
Of Greenwich Village

Pitiful drawings of
   images on an
   iron fence
   ranged there
    by selfbelieving
    artists
    with no hair
    and black berets
    showing green seas
    eating at rock
    and Pleiades
    of Time

Pestiferating at moon squid
  Salt flat tip fly toe
    tat   sand traps
  With cigar smoking interesteds
      puffing at the
        stroll

I mean sincerely
  naive sailors buying prints
Women with red banjos
   On their handbags
   And arts handicrafty
   Slow shuffling
   art-ers of Washington Sq
    Passing in what they think
   Is a happy June afternoon
Good God the Sorrow
   They dont even listen to me when
   I try to tell them they will die

They say "Of course I know
I'll die, why should you mention
It now—Why should I worry
About it—it'll happen
  It'll happen—Now
  I want a good time—
  Excuse me—
  It's a beautiful happy June
  Afternoon I want to walk in—

Why are you so tragic & gloomy?"
And on the corner at the
     Pony Stables
Of Sixth Ave & 4th
Sits Bodhisattva Meditating
In Hobo Rags
 Praying at Joe Gould's chair
For the Emancipation

Of the shufflers passing by,
Immovable in Meditation
He offers his hand & feet
  To the passers by
And nobody believes

That there's nothing to believe in.
Listen to Me.
There is no sidewalk artshow
   No strollers are there

No poem here, no June
   afternoon of Oh
But only   Imagelessness
Unrepresented on the iron fence
Of bald artists
   With black berets
   Passing by
   One moment less than this
Is future Nothingness Already

The Chess men are silent, assembling
Ready for funny war—
Voices of Washington Sq Blues
   Rise to my Bodhisattva Poem
      Window
  I will describe them:
  E y t k e y ee
    S a   l a o s o
      F r up t urt

Etc.
No need, no words to
    describe
The sound of Ignorance—
They are strolling to
    their death
Watching the Pictures of Hell
Eating Ice Cream
    of Ignorance
On wood sticks

That were once sincere
  in trees—
 But I cant write, poetry,
  just prose

I mean
 This is prose
  Not poetry
   But I want
    To be sincere

CANTO DOS

While overhead is the perfect blue
  emptiness of the sky
 With its imaginary balloons
   of false sight
 Flying around in it
   like Tathagata Flying Saucers
 These poor ignorant things
   mill on sidewalks
 Looking at pitiful pictures
   of what they think

Is reality
And one
  a Negro with curls
Even has a camera
 to photograph
The pictures
And Jelly Roll Man
Pops his Billy Bell
 Good Humor for Sale—
W Somerset Maugham
   is on my bed

An ignorant storyteller
  millionaire queer
But Ezra Pound
 he crazy—
As the perfect sky
 beginninglessly pure
Thinglessly perfect
 waits already
They pass in multiplicity

Parading among Images
Images   Images   Looking
    Looking—
And everybody's turning around
     & pointing—
  Nobody looks up
        and In
  Nor listens to Samantabhadra's
  Unceasing Compassion

No Sound Still
    S s s s t t
    Seethe
    Of Sea Blue Moon
    Holy X-Jack
      Miracle
      Night—
    Instead, yank & yucker
    For pits & pops

Look for crashes
  Pictures
   Squares
     Explosions
       Birth
         Death
           Legs
 I know, sweet hero,
Enlightenment has Come
    Rest in Still

In the Sun Think
    Think Not
 Think no more Lines—
Straw hat, hands aback
     Classed

He exam in a tein distinct
    Rome prints—
Trees prurp
    and saw—

The Chessplayers Wont End
   Still they sit
   Millions of hats
  In underwater foliage
   Over marble games
   The Greeks of Chess
    Plot the Pop
    of Mate
     King Queen

—I know their game,
   their elephant with the pillar
  With the pearl in it,
    their gory bishops
      And Vital Pawns—
      Their devout frontline
      Sacrificial pawn shops
      Their Stately king

Who is so tall
  Their Virgin Queen
    Pree ing to Knave
   the Night Knot
—Their Bhagavad Gitas
   of Ignorance,
   Krishna's advice,

Comma,
The game begins—
  But hidden Buddha
Nowhere to be seen
    But everywhere

In air atoms
In balloon atoms
In imaginary sight atoms
In people atoms

In people atoms
Again
  In image atoms
  In me & you atoms
  In atom bone atoms
  Like the sky
    Already waits
    For us eyes open to
      —Pawn fell

Horse reared
  Mate Kiked Cattle
  And Boom! Cop
      shot Bates—
  Cru put Two—
    Out—I cried—
    Pound Pomed—
    Jean-Louis,
      Go home, Man.

I mean.—
  As solid as anything
  Is this reality of images
  In the imageless essence,
  Neither of em'll quit
  —So tho I am wise
  I have to wait like
    anyotherfool

CANTO TRES

Lets forget the strollers
  Forget the scene
Lets close our eyes
  Let me Instruct Thee
    Here is dark milk
      Here is our Sweet Mahameru
        Who will Coo
        To You Too

As he did to me
One night at three
When I w k e l t
      P l e e
  knelt to See
  Realit ee
    And I said
  'Wilt thou protect me
        for ' ver ?'

And he in his throatless
    deep mother hole
  Replied 'H   o   m'
  (Pauvre Ange)
  Mahameru
      Tathagata of Mercy
See
 He
    Now
        in dark escrow

  In the middleless dark
of eyelids' lash obliviso
  so
    Among rains of Transcendent
        Pity

Abides since Ever
  Before Evermore ness
of Thusness Imagined
O Maha   Meru

O Mountain Sumeru
  O Mountain of Gold
    O Holy Gold
      O Room of Gold
        O Sweet peace
          rememberance
        O Navalit Yuku

Of sweet cactus
  Thorn of No Time
—Ply me onward
  like boat
   thru this Sea
  Safe to Shore
  Ulysses never Sore
—Bless me Gerard
  Bless thee, Living

I shall pray for all
  sentient human
 & otherwise sentient
 beings here & everywhere
 now—

No names
  Not even faces
  One Pity
    One Milk
      One Lovelight
          s   a   v   e

*

DESOLATION BLUES

1ST CHORUS

I stand on my head on Desolation Peak
And see that the world is hanging
Into an ocean of endless space
The mountains dripping rock by rock
Like bubbles in the void
And tending where they want—
That at night the shooting stars
Are swimming up to meet us
Yearning from the bottom black
  But never make it, alas—
  That we walk around clung
  To earth
  Like beetles with big brains
Ignorant of where we are, how,
What, & upsidedown like fools,
  Talking of governments & history,
—But Mount Hozomeen
The most beautiful mountain I ever seen,
Does nothing but sit & be a mountain,
A mess of double pointed rock
Hanging pouring into space
  O frightful silent endless space
—Everything goes to the head
  Of the hanging bubble, with men
  The juice is in the head—
  So mountain peaks are points
  Of rocky liquid yearning

2ND CHORUS

Mountains have skin, said Peter
    Orlovsky of San Francisco—
And gorges shoot up clouds of mist
  That look like planet smoke—
Dead trees, artistic as a cottage
    on Truro,
  Look like goat horns off a rock,
—Alpine firs turn evergreen browns
By August First when summer's dead
At high elevations—the creeks roar
  And cataracts tumble pouring
  But it's all upsidedown & strange
—Why do I sit here crosslegged
On this steaming rocky surface
Of a planet called earth
Scribbling with a pencil
Unmusical songs called songs
And why worry my juicy head
And rail my bony hand at words
  And look around for more
    And nothing means nothing
      as of yore?—
  T s the primordial essence
  Manifesting forms, of happy
  And unhappy, stuff & no-stuff,
    Matter & space, phenomena
    Front & noumena behind,
    Out of exuberant nothingness

3RD CHORUS

Yet birds mumble in the morning,
And raccoons tumble down the draws,
  I saw one hit by his own rock
  In a lil raccoon avalankey—
  And firs point as ever
             to infinity,
Their fine points top points too,
—Birds squeak like mice,
  and moonlight bucks & does
Graze in my yard like cows
With big shootable flanks,
  And hooves of eternity, clatter
    on the rocks,
  Run away when I open the door,
  Down the hill, like silly frightened
    schoolteachers—
Chipmunks are well named—
Bears & abominable snowmen
I have not yet seen—
    Proud a that line—
Rock slides take generations to form,
  I try to rush it along—
  No rain in a month, nor yet
    a month, within a month—
  The beaked furthereal pine
    points at a crazy
Upsidedown mid morning moon
    as delicate
As a slide, like snow

4TH CHORUS

All the worries that've plagued
   everybody since Moses, Homer,
Sappho, Uparli, Cannibals and
    Patawatamkonalokunopuh
Are worrin and playin me
   on this mount of mystery—
I've T S Elioted all the fogs,
   Faulknered all the stone,
Balanced nothing gainst something,
   played solitaire, smoked,
Brought bashing sticks to midnight
    frightful long tailed rats
 And ranted at mosquitos,
 And remembered my mother
   her sweet labors of home
 And the cold eyed sister
   who made a bum outa me,
 And friends, & goodtimes,
   & prayed & gave up prayer,
And pondered history, myths,
   stories, artistic plans, plays,
French movies, phalanxes
   of disordered human crazy
   Thought, & still it's upsidedown—
   Silent—stiff—wont yield—
   Wont tell—A big empty
    Puppet stage, with rock

5TH CHORUS

Distant valleys in Canada
    look like they'd beckon
    but I know better,—
I yearn for the flatlands again,
   the gentle hill,—
At 4 PM the clouds of hope
Are horizon salmon floaters
Full of strange promise
    abstracted from the golden age
    in my breast—
Patches of snow dont do anything
    but be
Patches of snow, till they melt,
And then water, it's nothing
    but water
Till sun evaporates, then mist,
It's (as I look) nothing but mist
As it rises ululatory responding
    to every shift of wind,
  And will be mist, and will be
Mist,
  And ants are nothing but just
    ants,
    And rocks'll sit where they are
      forever
Lessn I move em, throw em
    down the gorge,
And then they spit a minute

6TH CHORUS

I just dont understand—
tho mist'll be mist till
Heavens obdure, tho man'll
Be man till heavens obdure
Or hells obscure   I just
dont
I just dont
Dont
Understand
        I dont—
    I want to know—soon's a do
I dont understand—if I said:
"I dont care" I understand—
I understand that
            it doesnt matter.
Still the birdy clings, to earth,
He dont go silent on me,
I dont stop writing,
  I dont stop living,
What a fool,—bust the bird.
  The only thing that ever happens
        to Hozomeen
  Is that he'll get a wreath
    of clouds
  Every now & then
        & breed to revel
  Without moving a mighty shoulder
—I envy him his rock

7TH CHORUS

But I want to live, I want
    to get down
Off this Chinese Han Shan hill
    and make it
To the city & walk the streets
And drink good wine
        (Christian Brothers Port)
Or whiskey (Early Times
            or Old Grand Dad)
    And go to Chinese Movies
            on Saturday Afternoon
    And buy presents in the window
    and watch the dust gather
    On little stationary toys
    In celluloid windows of children
And go to the vast markets
    And eat tortillas beans
            ice cream
    And crime—and banana splits
            and tea
    And benzedrine & broads—
            and waterfronts
    And plays & play marquees
            and Square Times
    And you—I'd like to celebrate
            upside
        Down in cities

8TH CHORUS

Once I saw a giant
                in a building

He's here now, bending
        over me,
Giant diamond gone insane.
Ta, the Golden Eternity,
        Ta Ta Ta Ta,
    Tathata, trumpet, Ta Ta,
    This giant diamond might
    Here is got some name'r other
    But *I dont know*
        I dont care
        and it makes no difference
    And now I'm wise.
    When the whole wide world
            is fast asleep I cry.
Let me offer you
        my reassuring profile
Saying, "It's okay, girl, we'll
    make it
Till the sun goes down forever
And until then what you got
            to lose
But the losing?   We're fallen
        angels
Who didnt believe
That nothing means nothing."

9TH CHORUS

We're hanging into the abyss
    of blue—
In it is nothing but innumerable
    and endless worlds
More numerous even (& the number
    of beings!)
Than all the rocks that cracked
  And became little rocks
    In all that rib of rock
    That extends from Alaska,
    Nay the Aleutian tips,
    Down through these High Cascades,
      Through to California & Ensenada,
      Down, through High Tepic, down
    To Tehuantepec, down,
    The rib, to Guatemala & on,
    Colombia, Andes, till the High
    Bottom Chilean & Tierra
        del Fuego
    O yoi   yoi
    And on around to Siberia—
In other words, & all the grains
    of sand that comprise
   A rock, and all the grains
    of atomstuff therein,
  More worlds than that
     in the empty blue sea
We hang in, upsidedown,
—Too much to be real

10TH CHORUS

But it's real
   it's as real as the squares
   on this page
And as real as my sore ass
   sitting on a rock
And as real as hand, sun,
    pencil, knee,
Ant, breezed, stick,
   water, tree, color,
   peeop, birdfeather,
   snag, smoke,
   haze, goat,
   appearance
   and low crazed cloud
And dream of the Far Northwest
 And the little mounted policeman
Of my dreams on a ridge—
    Not an Indian in sight—
Real, real as fog in London town
   and croissants in Paris
   and swchernepetchzels
   in Prienna
 And Praha Maha Fuckit
 —Real, real,
   unreal,
   deal,
   Zeal,
 I say, dont care if it's real
    or unreal, I'se

11TH CHORUS

And if you dont like the tone
   of my poems
You can go jump in the lake.
I have been empowered
   to lay my hand
On your shoulder
    and remind you
That you are utterly free,
Free as empty space.
You dont have to be famous,
    dont have to be perfect,
 Dont have to work,
     dont have to marry,
Dont have to carry burdens,
    dont have to gnaw & kneel,

    the taste
     of rain—
   Why kneel?

Dont even have to sit,
    Hozomeen,
Like an endless rock camp
    go ahead & blow,

Explode & go,
    I wont say nothin,
    neither this rock,
  And my outhouse doesnt care,
    And I got no body

12TH CHORUS

Little weird flower,
    why did you grow?
Who planted you
        on this god damned hill?
Who asked you to grow?
  Why dont you go?
  What's wrong with yr. orange tips?
  I was under the impression
      that you were sposed to be
      some kind of perfect nature.
Oh, you are?
        Just jiggle in the wind. I see.
  At yr feet I see a nosegay
      bou kay
  Of seven little purple apes
    who dint grow so high
And a sister of yours
    further down the precipice—
    and your whole family
     to the left—
I thot last week
    you were funeral bouquets
    for me
    that never askt
    to be born
    or die
  But now I guess
     I'm just talkin
     thru my
      empty head

ORIZABA 210 BLUES

1ST CHORUS

Ah monstrous
sweet monsters,
who spawned
thee chalk?
 God? Who
 Godded me?
 Who me'd
 God, chalk'd
 Thought, &
 Me sank
 Down
 To
 Fall

A tché tché tcha
    hoot ee
Wheet wha you—

Sweet monstranot love
By momma dears

Hey

Call God the Mother
To stop this fight

2ND CHORUS

Someday you'll be lying
there in a nice trance
and suddenly a hot
soapy brush will be
applied to your face
—it'll be unwelcome
—someday the
undertaker'll shave you

*

I almost called these poems
Pickpocket Blues
because they are the repetition
                              by memory
                    of earlier poems
                              stolen from me
            b y   t w e l v e   t h i e v e s

3RD CHORUS

Ah monster sweet monster
Who spawned all this God
A Marva Ah Marvaila
Ah Marva Marvay
Ah marve   Ah Me
Ah John O Ah John
Oka John—
Where do you worka
John—Ah John,
How do you William the
Conqueror this morning
With your height old otay
—Nay, sight less worse,
Urp, the spur that did nape
At the wick the whack
Of the horse's piniard, urt,
So up heaved Pegasus
To rape the Sirens

And Black Bastards Hold Out their Arms

4TH CHORUS

One was called Boston Kitty—
He was a one-whack artist
Hold down the rope & the boy
And slip his villons i the store
—Oy—

This turp then, he was smart,
His wife was bloomer-hiding
Dress-thief, best, New York,
—Oir—

Ay
May the Wild Queen that Whanged
All the men with pipes
And ironingboard trays, i the
Movie bout paird?—
Waird!
Haird all about it in Dawson
Lass night, boys was tellin
The stove of the night
Hair—Robert Olson
Me that, Mrs Blake

5TH CHORUS

Pollyanna me that, Matt
Baker me Mary me Eddy
somethin bout life,—
Feed me T bone steaks
Off cows was allowed
Was allowed to be et
By men and maids
And Pomfranet

Poignardi me that,
hurt,—slip me the knife
in the chest, het—
they'll cut off my arms
and my losen legs
And my Peter Orlovsky
Clasel soul shall say:
Oido me no mo

6TH CHORUS

Ah moidnous two movies
Was railroad and et

Ah turpitude & turpentine
And serpentine & pine

Ah me star-veil
    that I see
Majesticking mightily
    on the rail
Of heaven-hailward
    high's moitang

Montana, me mountain,
Me Madonna, me high
Me most marvelous marvel
That held over the pie
Me sky of the Denver
Platte alley below

Me that me, me that me,
Me that me no more

7TH CHORUS

Brang!—blong!—trucks
Break glass i the dog barking
Street—dwang, wur,
Ta ta ta
    ta ta
Me that was weaned in the
    heaven's machine
Me that was wailed
    in the wild bar
called fence
Me that repeated & petered
The meter & lost 2 cents
Me that was fined
To be hined
And refined
        Ay
            Me that was
            Whoo ee
            The owl
            On the fence

8TH CHORUS

Me that was eyed
And betied by the eyes
In the glasses, In the Place,
In the night, brown beer,
Me that was maitled
And draitled and dragged
Me that was xarmined
By Murder Machree
Me that was blarnied
By Mary Carney
Me that was loved
Me that was hay
Me that the sunshine
Burned out every day
Me that was spotted
And beshatted
 By Marcus Magee

9TH CHORUS

Hey listen you poetry audiences
If you dont shut up
And listen to the potry,
See, we'll get a guy at the gate
To bar all potry haters
Forevermore

Then, if you dont like the subject
Of the poem that the poit
Is readin, geen, why dont
You try Marlon Brando
Who'll open your eyes
With his cry

James Dean is dead?—
Aint we all?
  Who aint dead—

John Barrymore is dead

Naw, San Francisco is dead
—San Francisco is bleat
  With the fog
(And the fences are cold)

10TH CHORUS

Old, San Francisco so old,
Shining garden on the end of the gate
Great plastic garden
Full of poets and hate

Fine wild bar place with high
Flootin dandies, Portugese,
Philippino, and just plain
Ole Dandy, Mandy tendin
The bar in the Brothers McCoy
On Sixth Street near Mission,
And Old Whitecap Sailor
Goes lonely the road
And Market Street on Sunday
There's no body broad
And O I see cliffside
With electrical magic
Message it me gives out
And sending Einstein
Me n McCorkle sit there
Eating in the Dharma

11TH CHORUS

We booted and we brained
Every seedy wet cold hill
And walked by rubber gardens
Behind telephones of shame
And came out mid the flowers
Of Heaven's O Gate

We treed every boner
Kited and committed
Longtailed and selffloored
And worked 78 to Del Monte
And back

Crashed Lux Perpetua
And tied up the mate
And dumped him down
In Chinatown
To Vegetate
So's cooks could clew garbage
And discover entrails
of babies made by Negresses
Against fences of taxis

12TH CHORUS

Soft!—the mysteries lie
In Eglantine

And Tathagata Nous Dit
Toujours, pas d secour,
    Pas d secour

Soft—pie-tailed bird-dog
Sing Song Charley the Poet
From High Masquerade
Is about to shake the rain
From his empty head
And deliver a blurbery statement
About bubbles and balloons

Balloons   O balloons
BALLOONS   BALLOONS
BALLOONS O BALLOONS
BAL
LOONS
B A L L O O N S

13TH CHORUS

When the rain falls on the Concord
And grapes are growing in New Hampshire
Mud hides wine bottles of green
And gay delight—When it rains
In Mexico, Oi Oi Oi, the swish
And plump and drenching Zapoteca
Big fat lump cacti growing in the night
Slipslop the sleeps of cats by the fence
And "Alms my youth!" cry women
To the passing Americano Oi—

Hate and oido, Old San Francisco's
Going to go—

Red, white and black, and blue
The pistil was tender when vines
Hund and daundered explosives
Of surrealistic pensioners

Dishrags have faces
Flashlights have hate
Pine trees are sweetest
To sit and meditate
The Holy Virgin of Heaven
Saw us in the rainy first morning

14TH CHORUS

Lost me Juju beads in the woods
And stood on dry stumps
    and looked around
And Lightning Creek morely roared
And wow the wild Jack Mountain
Abominable Snowman rooted
    in a stump
Even throwing football shadow
When games is ranging in the sky
Ah Gary,—would sweet Japan
Her gardens allay me
And make end sweet perfidy
—Full belly make you say
               nice things—
When rice bowl filled, Buddha frown
I' the West, because Wall of China
Has no holds

Holdfast to temple mountain chain
Throw away the halfdollars
Big and round, & wad of gum,
And flashlight lamp—& paint—
Go be shaved head monster
In a cave—No, tea ceremony
Beneath a sweet pine tree
          (Oi?)

15TH CHORUS

The little birds that live on the tree
In South America
Under clouds that make faces at me
Last night beautiful faces
Mad Dog McGoy of Heaven's
White Office, was sheening
His ocean spray at me
With holes for eyes
And every kind majesty—
Mocking at faces at me,
O me,—gingerale we drank
In Montreal when Errgang was young
And Wagner bleeded on the dump
And the dust of defeat perfidy
Was as fine as it is now
In the skies of untouchable dust
 And Klings of the rooftop
 Church variety—
 My moity

16TH CHORUS

Auro Boralis Shomoheen
In the ancient blue Buick
Machine that cankers the highway
With Alice fat Queens, cards
Indexes burning, mapping machines,
Partings sweet sorrow
But O my patine

O my patinat pinkplat Mexican
   Canvas for oil in boil
Marrico—hash marsh m draw
The greenhouse bong eater from
fence N'awrleans, that—

Bat and be ready, Jesus is steady,
Score's eight to one, none,
Bone was the batter for McGoy
Poy—
         Used as this ditties
         for mopping the kitties
         in dream's afternoon
         when nap was a drape

17TH CHORUS

"Jamac!   Jamac!
De bambi   de bambi
Jamac   jamac!"

 And elegant old quorums
        of fortified priests
  sighed

De bambi de bambi jamac
Jamac, and eldertwine
old tweedies fighted the prize

"Parrac!   Motak!
Pastamak   arrac!
     Arrash!
     Crrash!"

Part art tee
  tea symphony
ceremonious old bonious
   me love you
   me

18TH CHORUS

Henry Regalado, l'hero de la
Bataille de Patenaud

God and all the other little people

Esmack, esmack, I esmacka
You on the kisser you too
I thrun nobody oud dis joint
Since Roosevelt had all his joints

And Buddy I knowed
That old Patenaude
Was a fraude from the start,
Tonio me Kruger you that,
Hat—
Pat was the rat that had the hat

Mash patinaud
Crash toutes les shows
Grange toutes les villes
    les jilles
Mange toutes les filles

19TH CHORUS

The diamond that cuts through
To the other view
That I painted all white for you
I edited your rough stone,
Produced a diamond show,
Elephantine was the mine
Eglantine adamant and mad
  And madly adamantine
  My Allah you mine,
  The diamond of Dipankar
  The prime ripe wreak havoc
  Buddha pra-teeth torn
  Mouth Ya-Hoi-Ya-Hai
  Pastumintapaling porpitoi
  Turnpot of biled pata taters
  Smater Gater the Mater
  O'Shay, rife was the weather
  Was singin was gay,
  Rape were the weathers
  In heaven's O Shay

20TH CHORUS

Old buddy aint you gonna stay by me?
Didnt we say I'd die by a lonesome tree
And you come and dont cut me down
But I'm lying as I be
Under a deathsome tree
Under a headache cross
Under a powerful boss
Under a hoss
      (my kingdom for a hoss
        a hoss
    fork a hoss and head
    for ole Mexico)
Joe, aint you my buddy thee?
And stay by me, when I fall & die
In the apricot field
   And you, blue moon, what you doon
   Shining in the sky
   With a glass of port wine
   In your eye
—Ladies, let fall your drapes
and we'll have an evening
of interesting rapes
      inneresting rapes

21ST CHORUS

Let fall the interesting fall
And I lie and be as I be

He stayed up in my case
    for quite awhile

Tremendous pace—He was
A petty thief or he'd sell junk
One or the other

I did my best to keep him from
    selling junk

French fag from Montreal
Hid the capsules up his ass
And took em out in a restaurant
On Broadway and Ninety Sixth

And I went to Eighty Sixth
  Those girls hit up on me
  "Man is here!"
And I bought four more caps

And the fag went home with a girl
    What a beautiful shape
    that woman had

22ND CHORUS

Ha well dear and Ah Men
The wee girl that was comin again
She was for the books
  The Ursula plea
  That I could not take

O you better baike
  O you better bake
  A better cake than this
O you better Miss
Yes you better miss
When the thing never will kwiss

O sweetheart and okay
Here's hopin we'll all be away
  It was great fun
But it was just one a
    those tings

23RD CHORUS

Dom dum dom domry
Dom—dom—hahem—
Sum—(creeeeee!)—Hnf—
Shh—Hnf—Shh—Haf
Shhh—Shhh—Hiffff—
—Ma—
Snffff—(bing bring, se ting)
—"Yo conee na nache"—
D ding—d ding—d-ding—
Cramp!—O ya ta dee
—ker blum—kheum—
Hnffff—drrrrrrrr—drosh—
Pepock—Shiffle—t bda—
Want a piece a bread
    No
Jack? Hnff—Ta ra ta ra fuee
—Te wa ta ra teur—
Grrr—he na pa powa shetaw—
   Tck tick tick Today is Sunday

24TH CHORUS

Eternally the lightning runs
Through form after form formless
In positive and negative repose

It makes no difference that your uncle
Was black with sufferance & bile,
The whild childscriming skies will
Always be the muchacho same

Much words been written about it
The message from infinite
That will be was brought to us
Is one
But because it has no name
We can only call it Bibit
    "It was Liebernaut who had
      the dream of uncovering Carthage"
The snow in the sea mountains

25TH CHORUS

In Egypt under rosebushes
Fifi's fruits & sweets

My Egyptian connection's
Gonna be late, the conductor
Wouldnt take my change

The Egyptian conductor
Wouldnt nod

Sandalwood and piss and pulque
Burning in every door,
Mighty Marabuda River
Flows along

Sampans and river thieves
And woodsplitters and blind
Thieves' Markets & imbeciles
"See Milan and see the world"

Heppatity the twat kid
Hatted by the racetrack
Horses' moon barns
spun on a gibbee
For lying alone

26TH CHORUS

My poems were stolen
    by Fellaheen Thieves
In the city of the midnight

The title was "Fellaheen Blues"
And justice is done to Rome

I'll never see them again
Learn what sweet development
I'd harbored up to meditate
All's left now
       is these hateful
       New Fallaheen Blues
       which mean nothing
       and I hate them
In the other book I cried
Ah-da   Ah-da
  the parturient spinsters
  that prate i the dining hill
  Are having blue venison
  To goose their old hyms
    Og

27TH CHORUS

But I'll tell you—electricity
Runs through all these forms
And we call it electricity
And notice the forms
But what's hoppen in nothin
Is wha hoppen in nothin
   See?
      The butchers a de Bronx
      Ourter now dat

—the late night tweed diners
Italian restaurants on Bleecker
that sing in the staring blue street
with cigarettes of legs
   Ourter know dat
The wild outflow wow open
O gate of golden honey
Hopin hill up above
And below & within
The kin, aye, my,
What a roseate balloon
For lovers of kin

28TH CHORUS

Part of the morning stars
   The moon and the mail
The ravenous X, the raving ache,
—the moon Sittle La
Pottle, teh, teh, teh,—
The tatata of thusness
Twatting everywhere—

   The poets in owlish old rooms
   who write bent over words
   know that words were invented
   Because nothing was nothing

In use of words, use words,
the X and the blank
And the Emperor's white page
And the last of the Bulls
Before spring operates
Are all lotsa nothin
   which we got anyway
So we'll deal in the night
   in the market of words

29TH CHORUS

And he sits embrowned
   in a brown chest
Before the palish priests

And he points delicately
   at the sky
With palm and forefinger

And's got a halo
   of gate black

And's got a hawknosed
   watcher who loves to hate

But has learned to meditate
   It do no good to hate

So watches, roseate laurel
   on head
In back of Prince Avolokitesvar
   Who moos with snow hand
And laces with pearls
   the sea's majesty

30TH CHORUS

The little bug thrasheth
                    on the table
Hungry to burn in the candle
    of flames
Jerks at the gate-bottoms
    of wax cold hide
Albions and Albans
    to his little sight
Leaps to be browned
    in the roast rite
Soars & tries to reach
    dizzy height
Falls in the temples
    and quivers & slaps
Playin like a schoolboy
    in the valleys
Of silver & ivory hate

31ST CHORUS

I

I had a slouch hat too one time
The old slouch hat
I just keep walkin around
And he keeps walkin around with me
Around and round that necktie
   counter we went
When it rained I wore my old
     slouch hat

It was a good felt that
   I had to carry through many
   rainy day, late fall
   and the early spring

Perhaps it was a rainy day
And the house dick mighta saw
My hat
       Each tie on that ring
        Worth six bucks, Brooks Brothers,
        Sixty bucks wortha ties
Slacks with peculiarities
I couldnt even find a pair of slacks
I thought it was suitable to wear

32ND CHORUS

II

Wrapped one pair around me
And pinned it with a safety pin
And pulled up my trousers and
  Went out looked at myself in the mirror
      'O no, those wont do'
      And I walked out

Wrap the slacks around my waist

Took two other pair
    went to the mirror
  threw them at the salesman
'No those wont do—good
    afternoon' and walked out

The slouch hat I got at Harvard
    Club, Yale Club, Princeton Club
    one or the other
    Dartmouth Club
    University Club

Always barred the Yatch Club
    because it was a little over
    my kin

33RD CHORUS

III

The doorman knew that only
    Mr Astor   Mr Vanderbilt
    Mr Whitney belonged

He couldnt say 'Good morning
    Mister Astor' because
    he knew I wasnt Mister
    Astor

I always figured a way to heel
    into those other clubs

Not only a member of Who's
    Who but a Who's Who
    also have to be a member
    of Who's Who in New York
    in the special clique of Who's

Hoo—slouch hat!

  I get in the Athletic Club
  many time

34TH CHORUS

IV

And I'd go up in the Billiard Room
And I would wander back around
The room, hands in back,
And every coat rack I backed
Up against feel for the wallet
      One day I walked
      Outa there with ten wallets

Bellboy lookin me over
Pretty soon a very dignified looking
   gentleman came up and buzzed
   the bell boy

He says "Who?" and I says
"Man told me his name, while
  We're drinkin at the bar,
  And told me to meet him
  In the billiard-room
  of the Athletic Club
I dont see him—so I best I
  better go"

35TH CHORUS

V

"Tell me about the old slouch
hat"

One of my numerous trips
to one of the numerous clubs
in New York City

The hat finally was left
in the hotel
which I had to leave
rather hurriedly one night
never to return
so the hat was given
to the castoffs of the hotel
which they collect
and rummage sells

May now be worn by one
Of the members of Skid Row

New York City—the Bowery

"I seen that hat
by moonlight"

36TH CHORUS

V I

I had a pointed mustache
   and I mean pointed
   half inch from here

Double breasted vest
    and a Derby hat
    and striped trousers
    English shoes, black,
    very pointed, they were
    Hannah Shoes

People on Broadway'd turn
    and look at me

The worst is yet to come
    I had a pince nez
    with a long black ribbon
    to my buttonhole

And I wore a carnation
    white or red

  Boy did I look like somethin

37TH CHORUS

VII

A year later I got caught
I was dressed differently
    and everything
But boy that mustache
    and that pince nez
    was really out of this world

I used that outfit six months
I finally had to pack it in
  because it was too well-worn

Pince nez was in a coat
  I stole
Mustache I grew in the
    sanitarium
While taking one of my
    numerous drug cures

My mother'd come to see me
    She says "Oh No!
    Cut it off!"
"I'm just havin a little fun, mother"

38TH CHORUS

VIII

Took it on the lam
And went to Canada

late at night I'm fulla
      morphine and I come down
      fulla goofballs too

This guy had ventriloquist doll
And he gave out this Texas Guinan
Routine "Hello Sucker, we
like your money as well
as anybody else's—s matter
of fact the bigger your roll
the more we take ya"

He used to get everybody
      interested with the doll
      and cutout silhouettes
      put stripes in your tie

Wound up in his room
      gave him a shot of morphine

39TH CHORUS

IX

Out on the highway I thumbed a ride
into Buffalo and I put the bum
on the guy for something to eat
—'Eat in my drugstore'—
So we went in the back
And he had corn on the cob
And boiled potatos, 'Say fellow
I always hear people talk
about morphine, what's it look
like?'—he shows me—he
had a key a cabinet and
he had bottles of hundreds
quartergrains halfgrains
pantapon delauddit everything
and soon as he tended
the customers I emptied the
bottles—got outa there pretty
quick, bought a safety pin
in Buffalo and took a shot
in the toilet

40TH CHORUS

X

Come out and saw a fellow
shaving, his coat hanging there,
hung my own coat and gave
his coat a brush of my hand,
felt his wallet, washed my hands,
and went out and took off
with the wallet

So I started out on a shoplifting
campaign in Buffalo
    wasnt very experienced at it

Started out with a topcoat
and I sold it in a taxicab stand

Next day I decided to get myself
some suits
    and I went up
    I had a suitbox
I walked about & put the suitbox
in one of the dressingrooms
    Looked & fooled in the mirror
    Went out, I hocked those two

41ST CHORUS

XI

Next day like a damn fool
go out to the same store
but I got a newspaper
instead of a suitbox
   thought I'd try
   a new routine

Two guys kinda watchin me
I went in wrapped myself up
two suits
     went in the elevator
     bottom gentleman
     tapped me on the arm
     'Will you come with me
                    please?'

And the County Jail they ate
breakfast and got oatmeal
with one spoonful of molasses,
for lunch stew, mostly bones,
Graveyard Stew, and for supper
   dinner at night
Beans—and you couldnt smoke

► • ◄

42ND CHORUS

Kayo Mullins is always yelling
and stealing old men's shoes
Moon comes home drunk, kerplunk,
Somebody hit him with a pisspot
Major Hoople's always harrumfing
Egad kaff kaff all that
Showing little kids fly kites right
And breaking windows of fame

Blemish me Lil Abner is gone
His brother is okay, Daisy Mae
and the Wolf-Gal

    Ah who cares?
    Subjects make me sick
    all I want is C'est Foi
    Hope one time
    bullshit in the tree

Hmmmmmmmmmmmmmmmm
I've had enough of foolin me
And making silly imagery
    Harrumph me katt
    I think I'll take off
    For Cat and fish

43RD CHORUS

Well & well well, so that's
The ancient fainter, the painter
Who tied up blue balloons
—Globas azul—and threw
Them asunder in the thunder
Of the ul—Ur—Obi—Ob-
Fuscate me no more travails,
Pardy hard, this rock mine
We're workin'll yield up diamond
                              hard

And then we'll cut thru conceptions
And come with answer pard

And what twill it be, sorry pard,
Aint never no mystery
Was imparted to me
Lessn you wanta try Roy McGoon
Who learned it in Innisfree

Or old Yow O Yeats, Blake,

We havent got the diamond tho
That freed Dipankara Buddha
In the Palaeolithic morning
And made him make faces
In Samapattis at me
    Let's free

44TH CHORUS

> High Cascades or Mexico—
> > headaches
> Travel everywhere

Forms and costumes and noses
All this changing literature
Cyrano de Bergerac, King
of the French underworld
King for a day, Henry V,
Falstaff his father, Henry IV,
Warlike stools frowning in
'We have no more use
 For your caisson iron,
 It's too fat
     and the water too vile,
     I'll vouch for the master
     but water your while
     had better be bile
     to judge from the green
     of the innocent liquid'
Reading, naught, words, styles
     The only thing matter is otay

45TH CHORUS

English Literature
   a School of Writing

French Literature
  was closed off

How tight the lips of Zola the
                       Master

Wont tell how he grips his pen
To consorts of learners

English, Old Shakespeare gathered
    bout him minor figures
    like Ben Jonson
    Maurie O'Tay
    Henry Fenelon
    And Molly O'Day

Irish Literature—that was
  where the brabac originated
  from
     Wood cracking in the sea

46TH CHORUS

And what is God?
The unspeakable, the untellable,
—

Rejoice in the Lamb, sang
   Christopher Smart, who
   drives me crazy, because
   he's so smart, and I'm
   so smart, and both of us
   are crazy

No,—what is God?
The impossible, the impeachable
Unimpeachable Prezi-dent
of the Pepsodent Universe
but with no body & no brain
no business and no tie
no candle and no high
no wise and no smart guy
no nothing, no no nothing,
no anything, no-word, yes-word,
everything, anything, God,
the guy that aint a guy,
the thing that cant be
and can
and is
and isnt

47TH CHORUS

Beverly Dickinson, wasnt it,
the distraught perfect poetess
who lived in New Hampshire
and wrote about roots & roses

Sweet old Beverly I remember her well
and her attic was fragrant,
her Attican divine
her storm bird
her fence story
her bee inside
her butterfly
her broom
her Majesty
the Queen

Said, "Emily Dickinson is as great
as Shakespeare sometimes,"
said T. S. Eliot's editor
Robert Giroux, swell fellow—
Her Attic divine, her antic,
—her

Sang in the blue hill
    her larks and mimes
And died all a silent
    in her prophecy tomb

48TH CHORUS

Dans son tombeau
Elle a gagnée
Toutes les lignes noires
D'Eternité

Que' s' trouve dans la terre
Quand qu'l mouille dans l'Hiver

Salonge!—Mompress!
Traboune!—Partance!

Elle a trouvée dejas
L'ange d'Archanciel
Couchez dans la mer
D'été d'nuée

Aye, oui, mes Anges toutes Francais
Mes tours d'ircanciel

Ma miel, mon or,
Mes ames deshonorées,
Mes troublages, mes lignes,
Mon vin sur la table
Ou sur le plancher

49TH CHORUS

Book of Dreams
(Written in dream language)
 Old Hosapho we wont let up
And hear me sing the
     hm—Ole Hosapho
     he wont let me record
     me dream language

Ooogh!   he upped & come back
       Ole Hosapho
But now he's down's
Gone down boy again

Hay Hosapho, say sumptin!
Hoy Hosapho, Roil!
  Nope Hosapho stay lead down
—A mani a Gloria—
    Tinkle tinkle laughter
    Dingle little pretties
       everything's happening everywhere

50TH CHORUS

My real choice was to go
to Princeton—I wanted
to be orange and black
on the football field

and orange Varsity letters
on black wool jackets
with buttons, and elm trees
and Sunday afternoon
the swish of the snow
and Einstein in his yard
and All's Well with
the Emily Dickinson world

And drive to New Hope
    for a drink
    or lobster

And take the sad train
on the platform of night
And ride into riot New York
On a Saturday Night
To go see Count Basie
Baying at the Lincoln
With Lester Otay Young
On Tenor Saxophone

51ST CHORUS

Boy, sa den du coeur, sa, le bon
vin—Mama, c'est'l'port
si fort, le vin divin—

Aye, oui, mais écoute—dans
les milieus de les nuits,
tu wé, sa den du coeur,
sa den du coeur

Ca fa du bien au beson

Besoigne?—Di mué pas la
besogne maudit, la bédenne,
maudit, la bédenne,
  sa fa du bien a bédenne
    pauvr' bédenne

A, y parle tu aussi bien
    q'ca
      a Milan
    les Italiens a gueules
Nous autres aussi on a une
belle lagne qui clacke

52ND CHORUS

Dog with mouths, in Navajoa,
bent down to the mud
and slippered shining entrails
in the morning Sinaloa sun
of a dead rabbit

Then the bus come and run
  it over, the rabbit, sullen
  dog skimpered off a minute,
  came back to repeat his
        refection

Oh well, shiney priests
      eat goodies
      in every store they see

Old Navajoa shit dog, you,
your goodies are the goodiest
goodies I ever did see, how
dog you shore look mad
when yer bayin

Hoo Hound-dog!
    dont eat that dead rabbit
    in front of my face raw
    —cook it a lil bit

53RD CHORUS

I had a scrap with a doctor
    one night
We were both drunk
I said "Just because you're
    a doctor you think you're
    so smart, if you're
    going to report me go
    ahead you prick"

And I fell off the stool
I was fulla goofballs

He went to the other doctor
"You better look this guy
up, he must be some kind
of a phoney"

Pony the pony the pony
the pra
Pony the pony the pony
the pra

54TH CHORUS

I got a grass jaw, boys,
I say, and knock out Ray
Robinson in the first minute
of the first round

Then they bring in Tiger Jones
because I made no bones
about how I was out to
Kayo Robinson, moonbless him

Tiger Jones comes on me all
fists, hard puncher, I got
nothing to do but retreat
or turn into grass, so
 I dance
 right in
 to his arms
  reach
and plow him all over
with crazy little punches
some of which are hard
  and we wake up

55TH CHORUS

Someday they'll have monuments
set up to reverend the mad
people of today in madhouses

As early pioneers in the knowing
that when you lose your reason
you attain highest perfect knowing

Which is devoid of predicates
such as: "I am, I will, I reason—"
—devoid of saying:-"I will do it"
—devoid

Devoid of insanity as well by virtue
    of no contact

But meanwhile these deterministic
doctors really do believe that mad
is mad—

And have erected a billion-dollar
religion to it, called, Psycho-medicine,
and ah—

Well we'll know the sanity
    of Ard Bar

In the morning, some time, alone

56TH CHORUS

Some'll go mad with numbers
Some'll go mad with words

Some'll pretend to lose reason
And lose reason anyway

Some wont, some'll be secret,
Some'll screw in long black
        rooms
With the fantastic short-haired
Beauty who lies on the bed
        listening

To Sinatra—some'll be candleflame
jiggling gently in the night

Some'll be racetrack operators,
some'll have soap in their pockets

Some'll sing in the Bronx Jail
and some wont sing in Riker's

Some'll come out of it
   with iron heads

Some'll wear coats
   and hard of it

57TH CHORUS

The monstrous jailer, he wouldnt let me
    outa that jailhouse—
        till I had smoked all the tea
        I could smoke, 'Finish up!'
        he said, & prodded me

And I gotta take big long hikes
    of draw on that cigarette tree

How'd I get outa that jail?
    By forgetting all about me

Which was the best rasperry tree
They ever ternevented in ole
Donnesfree
Cause I figure there's no difference
twixt me and dead dog mud
Made of bones and take your pick,
        sulphur or Innisfree

How'd they ever get that tap
        outa me?
Wasnt I tired givin?
        hard tap
Family tree.
I wasnt sweet givin.

58TH CHORUS

Las ombras vengadora
they say in little taco joints
when the shadows are coming
at about dusk-time, in Azteca,
modern Fellaheena Mexico,
Las ombras vengadora
Lass ombras venga dora
Most beautiful sound in the world
     hep!
  Swing up the team, bring up
    the gangs, say, didnt I yell
    at you a minute ago?

Hoy!
    Las ombras vengadora
    in little taco sad joints
    on Sunday Afternoon
    and fathers are home
    honoring their sons

59TH CHORUS

Fantasm crazam crazam
Joe Kennedy stops me on
    the sidewalk of the Immemorial
University—ack hook
You got your prick out.

I look down, no such thing

What are your two balls
doing hanging on the sidewalk?

I think I'll squat & shit—
We both squat facing each
    other on the campus
If ya know what I mean,
  cream, we squat
practice 'mitate Aristophanes
and sit there too laughing
and talking, Kennedy,
one of my first mature
    Irishmen

Face each other with feet
partly out, like in Esquire
the phonies showing their shoes
    Squat n Shit!

60TH CHORUS

I purified language early in my
young days, I purified & squatted
& beshitted on pages, sophomore,
on my typewriter, all the dirty
words I could think of
      squrify & squat & shit
And slit—and finally I'm
in history class & the professor
says 'Kerouac—what you
dreamin about?'
And I shhoudda said Ack—
Pack—Squrify and squat
and shit, who wants to hear
about the aniards and breast
plates of warriors of the
      Medieval Ages
I wanta know about the people
on the street, what they doin?
And what the high art
hark squambling in his quiet
 temple moonlit gambymoon
writing jingles & jongles
    for the pretties on the square

61ST CHORUS

Orizaba Rooftop blues
Listenin to the street news
Saturday night down there
Pleep! went the new little bike
    horn
As the cat pleeped it with his
Foot zinging the bike across
the fantastic bus-driven corners
Barging everywhere, he just angles
    and amples
      like Stan Getz on tenor
And swings around right around
    the fender okay

Orizaba rooftop, Orizaba Rooftop,
Blue, blue, blue
Blue's made of shiny everyway

Orizaba honk-honk, bus motors
Riding high for the clutch, tired,
Faces green on the benches,
Ikons in the corner
      Tails of little fenelet
      serpents hanging from the fender

Aik, motorcycle of no-cops,
Hotrods & Deans of Mexico,
Aik, aik, aik Mexico
      BORRACHO GUAPO BANJO

62ND CHORUS

Pipestoon the Ribber & wobbed
old ladies of shame. the same.
party twan twit Twittenden
Charley, 'Awfully good fuck!'
  he yells out the train window,
   to his waving host of the weekend,
'I say old chap, really!!'
and then Commando Poltroon
  comes platooning up in mudsplash,
  Monty, examining every commando
  standing naked in the rain,
    'That hurt?' whacking
    a guy on the rib, 'No
  sir,' 'Why not?'
     'Commando, sir'
Finally he comes to a man
with a long hardon, & whacks
it with his military crop
—with his baton—
'That hurt?'   'No sir'
        "Why not?"
  "Man behind me sir."

63RD CHORUS

The star is reflected in the puddle
    and the star dont care
    and the puddle dont care
Nothing is thinking
    not even the puddle poet

That's why "This Thinking Has Stopped"
Is the best way I know to imitate
    this starry state of affairs
    in puddles

Plass!   plash!—wait a minute!—
  wait a second buddy while I
  hock up old Desroches three
  sacrifices

      For each sacrifice you're reborn
      and you're only reborn once
      because there is only One
            Sin

Slatter me pet Charley, T-rod,
pettle pole and all, believes,
and goes rosing in the woods

Purt! Foley! Words! Names!
    Ahab, Starbuck & Pip
    Iago and Poltroon
    and Pipestaff the Ribber
—pain, pain, the no-name retoin

64TH CHORUS

On the street I seen three guys
standing talking quietly in the sun
and suddenly one guy leaps in pain
and whacks his fingers in the air
as he's burned his hand
        with a match
        lighting a butt

The other two guys dont even
        know this,
they go right on talking
        gesticulating with hands

I seen it, it was on San Jose
        Boulevard in St Joseph
        Missouri, nineteen thirty
        two

Them guys didnt even realize
pain is one thing, everywhere?

    Whai? Every golden
    sweetgirl come & befawdle
    her pillow in my hair
        and I dont care?
                Wha?

65TH CHORUS

JEWISH GOY IN N.Y.

Wha?   Whaddayou mean,
    there are ten thousands mysteries
    of me by the millions standing
    with hand-molded shows
    and sports jacket
    and no hair

bouncing along in one long corridor
of images in a mirror
    into infinity
    eternity
    call it what you will!

I know that!—You dont have
    pull that Buddha-stuff
    on me, Jack, I dont care

I've seen me in the picture
    stretched out everywhere
    it dont matter?
    Who cares!

I go to Lefty's & eat pastrami
    on Sunday afternoon,
    with mustard—I go hear
    some music at Carnegie Hall
    —I lay my wife—
    I sit on the bed, work

Who cares?   Wha?
    What's the moon got?

66TH CHORUS

What's the moon got but tunes?
Wha?   I dont care I'll talk
I'll stand right here talk
till doomsday, nobody care,
nobody say, who knows?   who
wants?   What's gonna free
what from what?   Shit!
  Gold! Girl! Honey! Call!
  What you will, call it,
  shit, I'll sit, I'll talk,
  I'll hang all day, because,
  it doesnt matter, you talk
  about it doesnt matter
  but you dont realize how
  doesnt-matter
  it really doesnt-matters,

        Wow man, I mean,

Sure, shoes, Shows, Hand
painted molds from azimuth
shoes, azipeth azipor
azinine blues, you got,
who cares, tsawright, eat,
pickles in the barrel—
    ——hail a cab—
        do what you want

67TH CHORUS

"It all goes down the same hole"
said Allen, eating cake & food
in a restaurant, with milk
in his coffee, no milk in the can,
no sense in the sour bottom
of that can

All goes up the same sky,
   all sucks on same air,
all plops drops impregnates
   and saves anywhere
The same limitation gentiles
   the crave for a show
on notwithstanding lost bibles
   dedicating the mystery
to a vain empty show,
'Vanity of Vanities,
    All is Vanity'
"Behold her breasts are like
   fawns"
   in the summer air,
Her eyes are like doves,
   skin like the tents
—Skin like the rents
in the heavenly air

68TH CHORUS

A murder   stern gird
A million dollar ba by
Ack
  Rowers of galleys,
  Candle lights,
  Hearners of yorn,
  Parturient ones,
  Poo,
  Patch art part tea
  Gart and band thee
  Harden thy garkle
  And get ye no purple kirtles
  Ere aye mice Burns
  Hands Mc Caedmon let loose
  His last tired crazy pom
      'Hung la terre,
      hang the twarrie,
    part de twaklockleme,
   gockle somackle magee'

  Down with the back rooms
  Of Dublin

69TH CHORUS

PRAYER

God, protect me!
 See that I dont defecate
  on the Holy See

See that I dont
 murder the bee

God! be kind!
 Free all your dedicate
  angels, for me

Or if not for me
 for anybody

God!   Hold fast!
 I'm dying in your arms
  delicately

Ah God be merciful
   to Princeton me

Ah God, alack a God,
 nobody farms
  amnesty

70TH CHORUS

I

There'll be no more ginger ale
for me
goodbye ginger ale
when I die
in Innisfree

That's where I'll go to die
to look and die
I'll never go there now

Because I've already told the boys
at the paper
the sound is crashing me

And they ate paper
And it was a paper party

But when the bell bonged toll,
And we all had to pay,
"Die in my arms, lamb,"
sang Rudy Vallee
from here to eternity

Die in my that's a beautiful arms,
    lad,
Die in my that's a beautiful arms,
    said God
To me

71ST CHORUS

II

That's just something
that isnt written
in Wells' history

That's something, Window Knock,
when you can make me
pray me

That'll do the reading
in London Library

And in Dublin I is free
To read
Old Innisfree

And then I'll read Finn
Again, and meet Magee
In a back alley

And get to know
    Donnelly
And the brothers Donnelly

That's where I'll be,
    My Arma Carney,
I'll be dyin
  down in Innisfree
Waiting for ye
Mary Carney

ORLANDA BLUES

1ST CHORUS

Le corp de la verité
pourre dans la terre

The body of truth
rots in the earth

nourriture dans la terre

Sanchez fourwinds bigtown,
dont wail that at me
 Fraserville Quebec
   comes back to me

 In the night sun sleep
 warm, store it in tanks

Blues of Old Virginia tree
     moonbottles over kiss time
    listener appeal
     Kissland
          Kissimee Florida
These are Orlanda Blues

2ND CHORUS

O Cross on my wall
   O body of Christ

When I was awright
   Saturday night

Little in your arms
   your thousands of years

In electric resist I wanted
   to soul the liking I saw
—*words*

      (musician pauses)

3RD CHORUS

This book is too nice for me
They made Clay Felker editor
of Esquire
Or Rust Hills one
and what ever happened to glass
and the joke about the Lord.

The Lord is my Agent.

My message is blah blah blah

My yort tackalitwingingly
   pasta vala tt, yea, p,
   my reurnent gollagigle
   dil plat most-rat, my
     erneealieing cralmaa
     tooth, ant, mop, sh,
   my devoid less 2 immensity
   secret muzning midnight,
   my whatzit
            you wanta
              know
                   Whatzit!
       Joy   Look out!

4TH CHORUS

Joy look in,
    look in,
        the pretty
           sin

    Loy, t a tt ct b
  I fooled with the long
  overload
    (wrong over road?)
  wronk

What a moistious wronk
we're in fair words,
  or is it wairds
   in your part
    of the
     Kelp,
    Laird

In Scotland we just throw
 the bones to the dogs
    & toast at the
       fireplace

5TH CHORUS

Well then let's have a toast
  I wonder if I can write
  poems just like Gregory
  Croso:—let's see:—
    The dead are dead,
      I'll resurrect them with
      this song,   O fall
        you fair held
        cities—
      (wood wood wood)
O held the fair held
    in the skinny bar!
    (the skinny bar held Indian
        sonofabitch)
    So North Mood wrote:—
    C o l t i n g—The Gregory
      says "Eels & gripplings
              in
              my
           eaves"

6TH CHORUS

Finally I was in Stockholm at last
Cold night
　Dark in Swedenborg

Zeldipeldi my junkey friend
　from N.Y. and Maldo
　Saldo the hot trumpeter
　　from Nigeria, turned on
　　in the cold room overlooking
　　black rooftops of winter,
　　　Sweden night skies February,
　　　Ommani pahdme hom

I wanted to catch a train
　　to the Capital

I was on a seacoast town,
　the name of it was Fidel
　or Fido
　　　wow, mominu,
　　　You dont know how far
　　　　that sky
　　　　　go

7TH CHORUS

Message from Orlanda:—
  You guys cant explore
  all of outer space, unless
  you want to spend
   a million million million
   million million million
    billion billion bullion
     bullion years at it
  —and when you gets
 . there, and you cant
    even get there, give my
     regards to Captain Bligh

And lissen, before you leave,
  how bringin my money
  with you to preserve
  in eternity, see, I
   can cash in when
   I get there & spend it
    on
        space
              travel

8TH CHORUS

Thats awright, space'll carry
us maybe like little eggs,
the buggy children work
 their way out
 to the surface
  of the egg,
   to the shell,
     they swim soft,
     & they get there
     & meet God
     The Shell
     The Shell
      hard & cold
       against the cold
             gray sun
              blood
               in
               your
             Father's
           Long Winter
           Underwear

    So sleep

9TH CHORUS

Me, I'm worried I'm a secret sinner
                and God
            Ole Tangerine
        I call   Him
    because one day I was settin
            under trees
                in
                a
            chair

And deciding what name
    to give to God, is it
    a personal God? & blam
    the little tangerine
            landed
            squarely
            on my
            head
        like Newton's
        underwear,

    & so I saw it personal
And I say the moral is simple

10TH CHORUS

But it landed right on the
    tippy tiptop
       of the sconce,
        Jazz,
        dazz,
  and that's why I believe
    (since it's all grinning
      in there)
        it was a little
        tap reminder

I dont *need* thunderclouds!

"Maybe Eden aint so
    lonesome as New England
used to be," said Emily
  Dickinson sitting with
    a tangerine in her hand

(They shipped it from Cuba)
 It was a great show
  Gasser!

11TH CHORUS

I guess God is alright
He'll take care of us

But there are perturbing roots
in these trees,
    that claw in earth
    & outa fingernails
      as long as Malaya
   eat up thru sucktubes
    the juice of the mother
     Terra Firma
     Mona Leisure

& these roots remind you
  of the roots in your grave
  I wish I could be cremated
  & sprung
       (to the wave),
  but Ah, hell, I donno
  I think I'll go to
    Sapplewhile
   & idle away the
  unfinished poem

12TH CHORUS

The evening silencius
Poetry
    is so pretty
 When you silence it like that

It's nice to pop pearl pages
the candlelight, you know,
   is dedicated to poets

Okay—dreaming fields—Blake
wants to hear the latest development
in the man the way the bleat
lambs bleakly blake it now
and that is soft,
        Ah William,
   I guess as soft as Spanish
   dreams, what was it Trappist
   said:— "Goats
          as
          soft
          as
          sleep"
 Something like that
   Farewell

13TH CHORUS

Jack Micheline
"Feet of children playing by
   the mill"—he didnt say
   hill—When tongue gets
   caught inside the lapels
   of the mouth, that's what
     I wanta hear—Like Fred
     Katz the cellist—or is
     it chellist?

"Tongue crucified, seven stitched"
     is pretty weird

Make it down to New Orleans
       one of these days
       says Moonlight Martin

"Maniac massacred" on account
       of "blinded on stone"
Wow, whatze mean?
Like Wolfe's Underground, mad dog
     choking in tunnels of hate
   "Spring has come
       yellow teeth & black hair"

14TH CHORUS

is exactly like the magnificent
haiku mailed to President
Eisenhower by Manosuke
Kambe
    "They have succeeded
        in shooting up a star
      And Spring is near"

    Yeah, where down yonder
   in you now Where

Now I'm getting to sound
  like a drearisome
   tangerine

Folks, read Jack Micheline,
      n doubt about it
He's a great poeit
And see?—read Gregory Corso
    too all about "bookies
     & chickenpluckers"
& Read Competition Ginsberg
   the maddest brain
    in poetry

15TH CHORUS

Ginsberg has a poet who
has a "great precise
 practical benevolence
   & new understanding,"
   and I have Jack
    Micheline, Steve Tropp,
    Steve White, and
   many other naked heads
   What I wrote first I kept,
     because I figure
                God moves
                the body hand
                because
                the body of the truth
                is a body
                 corruptible
                 in graves
                though
                nourishing,
                        O Schweitzer
                  Africa Trumpet!

16TH CHORUS

(And George Jones blows too!)

"Kneeling in the sun beside
the bright red mad beauties
of Street!" sings Corso

"I drag him into
myricolorous St Chapelle
Stained Glass marvel,"
sings Ginsberg

      Dont discourage
         the poets!

Sings Jack Micheline:
"And kiss the strangers
& plant the seeds of life among the dead"

  Because it's a distant
  hightone rail
"Flower of cities"

17TH CHORUS

And these sweet lines revive
the open poetry of hope
in old America
          long fish

And this sweet moth revised
  the entelechy
  in my endebechy
  in old pardodechy
  where Croo-Ba
  made it working
  boy girls in

He was hanged in the closet
  The King ate sliced sage
    John the Baptist had no head
    Jesus had nails in his skin
    The Neon's nailed to me
    I wish I were dead
    Or King of Ronald Colman
    country, or Kin to Sariputra
          Shakespeare, one

18TH CHORUS

Well, s'long as barrel womps we'll
    womp em on in, Used to write
    poems about Princeton boy rose

Also Baltimore bleedings
    & think rabbit plate
shit
  I wish I had
      a way
        to make
            Tuesday Sarah
              come by
                any day

With China throwup
      hadnt Puttered
      men with me

    but bile was free,
        & girl long blonde
          taffy pull

I guess best thing to do
    is to write to
    Blues Bessie

19TH CHORUS

I wonder what Emily's thinkin
in that groomus earth of
coral snakes & alligators
on the sidewalk, is she got down
  by Sunday in the Tomb, or
does time matter no blow out
bulbs of shame, Jesus, what
  shame in eyelid war life
  no shame at all in eyelid
  ant eat

  allied ant eat
What wars Bismarck plotted
  on accounta ambitious
  bishops, I dont know,
  what Colbert built
    for Mazarin slurp,
    or why French Blond
    Hero bombs black
      Arab dream in sand
    of Berber Ya ke
      Silhouette Blue men
    veil, kill me, I'se
    free

20TH CHORUS

Jazz killed itself
But dont let poetry kill itself
Dont be afraid
   of the cold night air

Dont listen to institutions
When you return manuscripts to
         brownstone
dont bow & scuffle
      for Edith Wharton pioneers
or ursula major nebraska prose
  just hang in your own backyard
            & laugh play pretty
               cake trombone
& if somebody gives you beads
   juju, jew, or otherwise,
sleep with em around your neck
Your dreams'll maybe better

   There's no rain,
         there's no me,
      I'm telling ya man
         sure as shit

21ST CHORUS

That cat's in paradise
The noise of automobile sigh
　　dont interfere with the knowing
　　of me or any paper party
　　　but's what smat smeldied
　　on hey-now,　Zulch!

Truth is, cry

Because the radar never was invented
could find paradise sound
or cat lost in the night
　　　　radarless
　　　radar-less
　　　　rad-arless
　　　radarle-ss

　　　　rrrrt
　　branged suitcases as a kid
　　& sang to Glenn Miller's
　　　Moonlight Serenade
　　　　　& Laid
　　　But O, Lord above,
　　　　　　have pity on my
　　　　　　　missin kitty

22ND CHORUS

Usta smear ma lips with whiskey
  Fred and open up the doors
  to make a joke—while
   women waited
   and Bert Lahr waited
   playing what he waited
    like Duke Ellington

used to sit staring at Seymour
who implied to me the swing
   of the music by his
      low crash
      high abidin
          shoulders,
        P a p,
   and what wow hoo?

T h o t l a t n a p e
   Compose Vehicle
    Special
    Banana
    Nine

23RD CHORUS

Bat bow
lack Jack
swing Bing
that's right!
Yes
backwards—wail—
You're gut okay man
swing on along
I don't care
I can do it
   too
Orlak + +
   see

24TH CHORUS

If you once
 for all good
  times
Man's fine,
   know
YOU KNOW

25TH CHORUS

My mind! even harder than
     my path, my freedom
     is in piano
O, wow, wild wow
   NBC OOO
        piano
Like Lee Konitz
        sky,
Yay, wow?
     Sluke!
Slow! Swing? THEN
     YOU GO—
That new tenor cat
made me drop my pencil,
     Elvin Jones

26TH CHORUS

Zoot Sims
  and his
   Johnny Williams
"This Happy Leaping Thing"
Kitty Drum Barry
Gray, you like cemetary
    swing?
"Big Xmas Seal"
Hockey teams—?
Al? —shape
lay, & the Elington
Good high school
    sex orgy
     girls
    in the woods
     of
     rape,
     nun dear

27TH CHORUS

The New Orleans New York
    Club
wishes to announce
    the opening
    of
    new sessions,
  & new fields, Daddio,

    Dave Brubeck's
     the swingingest

And I wish to say
Farewell
       to
         Al
         Smith

   Hello Dave

28TH CHORUS

For Minors Only
is the name of a new record
 all about trumpet
 & trimban

Zlap
        Peter Orlovsky
    is the cat to play to

You see dont you dig
        on all sides
        the wild sounds?
    and o the conceptions
        you made
            on
        Thursday
        afternoon

    trumpet man, dont blow
            that thing at me,
            blow it to
                    banana

29TH CHORUS

Timmy got back,
    soft Blakey lamb

Timmy got back
     & wrote rhymes

And we sat purring on the bed
    with Tammy

And made it 5 percent
    thousand

Times a day, swinging,
  we had sand,
 We had Gothic top
    Cathedral girls

  But O in Euniceburg
    they footballed
  Stupid me from Edgar
    Lear's interior
  Majesty

30TH CHORUS

No, this lamby bit
Is what I mean

O Orlando, O sweet

No Orlander phonecalls
   Georgia Flowerbranch

Lamby mean, William,
  Lamb dust?   Nnaaa!
Softy uglu flutey?
   Almost—

Pan flute Erdic
  Shook spear
  that Venusian cunt
  was neat when
    I'se a Nigger
      was
        a
        baby

31ST CHORUS

O Gary Snyder
  we work in many ways

In Montreal I suffered tile
  and rain

In Additional Christmas
  waylayed babes

In old crow Hotels
 full of blue babes
in pink dressinggowns
       down

  But O Gary Snyder,
     where'd you go, .
  What I meant was
     there you go

In Montreal I worked a manied-way

And, better than Old Post,
  I learned t'appreciate
    in many ways
     Montreal, Soulsville,
      and Drain

32ND CHORUS

Listening to a guy play
  tenor saxophone &
   keep the tune inside
    chords & structures,
     as sweetly as this,
      you'll experience
      the same
       fitly thrill
        you got from Mozart

It is pure musical beauty,
   like a musicale
    among wigs

People who dont understand
jazz are tone-deaf
   & dont understand
  what tone-deaf &
    simply deaf
    meant to Ludwig

33RD CHORUS

                van
                Beethoven

            *

    Goats as soft as break
            of day
    In swamp
        Mexico

            *

Can diamond cut iron?
  Diamond cuts glass
        glass links

  But can it cut
  An iron link?

  Nirvana means Cut-Link

If diamond dont cut glass
  or iron dont count,
                hey?
        maybe the Wisdom Vow
        o the Diamondcutter
        may have made it

34TH CHORUS

The only responsibility to a child
  is to feed, the rest is
  interference

    Can you just see
     a man arrested
      for letting his daughter
      fuck
         around the block
         anyway
         anywhere
       just so long as she got
       home to eat her
       dinner, he's telling
           the cops
          absolutely that

And the girl gets married?
  I have a bunch of stray cats
    in my yard

I wouldnt *have* a daughter

35TH CHORUS

Whattayouwanta have er for
　You wanta sling sperm
　　over her?
　Avin her now, ey you
　　old reprobate

Lissen, just keep that daughter
　　away from my knees
　　after she's thirteen

And between ten & that
　　tell her to lay off
　　the rough stuff

With boys you can play
　　as rough as you want,
　　but once ye spank em
　　they hate you forever

Oi Karamazov!

36TH CHORUS

O Apollo

Men

are the beautiful

The women miss cats

            Cads & rogues
                of Montreal all,

    or blue diers in deep pars
        asking for golfscore

But in any Case
            tsa united press

37TH CHORUS

Old dotin old fuck

There's this old man,
he come down this road
just a walking with some
  a whatyamaycallit
    in a big bottle

& I dont know what was in it
& it come night
& I was in my house
& here come this old man
      down the road
    drinking outa that bottle
      And there was Allen Wayne
    in his house

38TH CHORUS

& he had to hang this sheet
  on the clothesline

& that old man dropped
  that bottle in his
  yard

& that shu old man
  dropped that bottle
  down that road

  And that's all,
    Uncle Fred

39TH CHORUS

Maybe it's resting in the arms
    of Jesus,
  or just a cloudy windy day
In the trees

         *

But since there's an infinite
    amount of angels,
      and Infinite ends in no 's,'
     it must be
      one angel

Infinites Angels?

Maybe that bird that floats
hill belly on the wind up there,
  and that cat
    that pats
    in this grass,
  is the same
    Infinite
    Worldwide
     Angel

40TH CHORUS

A hard hearted old farmer
hidin his wine in the cellar

When he goes out he wears
earmuffs

He has a doublebitted axe
sharp enough
to shave shit

His people are all buried
  in the same cemetery,
   which is located
   under the doorstep
   where the boy
   couldnt get through
    from the tomb

41ST CHORUS

If we do battle,
  Monsieur,
And you lose,
  I gain nothing,
And if I lose,
   you gain
Satisfaction

This is what the peasant said
  when the aristocrat
  challenged him to a duel

Women move slowly
  but they dont stop

Europe, weep in your gloomy
    rain

I brought it to him
   so I could get you
      in Paradise

42ND CHORUS

Abraham, drinking water by the tents

Pacing up & down the soft sand
    under the stars

Worrying about Villages

Wondering if your vision was real
or just a foolish importunity
in your mind.
 Yet moving on in the morning anyway
    with the rattle of pack asses.

Abraham, the dew is in your beard
Abraham my eyes are open
  You are weird

    Abraham they've brought you
    Your rooftops are mended

    Your women bend no more
        their heads under the sleepy
        tentflap, & goats dont yew
        & cry nomo in the singsong
        tentvillage night

43RD CHORUS

Abraham I didnt write this right

44TH CHORUS

Dont ever come to Florida

A man was gettin up for work
   & reached under his bed
   in Kissimee
   and a coral snake
   bit him, February Florida
   (lookin for his shoes)

A little boy playin in his yard
was et by a alligator
    (true)

And an old lady dyin in her bed
   was et up by fire ants
   which found her
   clean from the yard

And my mother saw a lizard
    one foot long
    on the garbage pail
     that had big red eyes
 (The fire ants went in
      thru the mouth, man)

45TH CHORUS

There's a middlewestern prurience
about Greeks.—

Your little earth-nut, O potato
war, riots mama dears around
  papap's paternal root

  S i l k y b o o

 (o o !)

    Found the Sound

46TH CHORUS

Hollywood boy sing dog song
Dont be fooled by gun car
Or shine in hat of Sheriff
Cochise,
   or turn that dial,
   boy, you know whats happen
   to you when yard dog
   bit your fame

Yair, & dont sweep any leaves,
  Watch me play basketball
     I guess—

    In Inverness, where I'sa
    played hogball since
      your pappy skinned
         —Okay, old
           suit, see
           ya more

47TH CHORUS

Airplanes dropping barrels
  of shit on the White House
  On Roosevelt's very head
What do the women know
    of the wood?

All they gotta do is get drunk,
  Honorary Mayor

Up sprang the butcher boy
with the spring old man!

Why'st the fool play thou?

Because fools always follow.

  Followest what?

Because fooly are always follying?

    Nay, Sire, it was forgotten
  in that body's balconeer

48TH CHORUS

God ushered me into my house
What a batting champeen
    honorable American Navy
   Sweetheart God is to us
     Japanese Rigour Girls

Buy that, Moke!

  Dazz, I'ze innerested
   in drape fall circus
   and yo, yo got childrees
   pleak okomiko bonny
   sugar, ah, sweet,
dont let Robert Burns
  burn that cigar of yours
 Or mice lay men
   to diamondshine
    your kittlepee poopoo
     Grace,
      Otherwise purd
       Hurt
        New Year

49TH CHORUS

Way out
But not too way out

Barefaced wretch—
you're a pretty nice
barefaced wretch—
as bare faced wretches

go

T r u e   T o y !

Great day in the morning,

Ugh-y!

50TH CHORUS

Hollywood, if you want
little girls raped by sex
fiends, dont hint with
symbols, give it to me
  S t r a i g h t

Otto was pretty miserable
He chased little girls
   to rape in sawdust
  apartments yet unbuilt

He was a ugly big Otto
  but O when I was
   a little girl I loved
    all that

The lovely maniac
makes me smile

51ST CHORUS

Who is going to get rid
of his discriminating mind,
  which is the way to
  heaven, when he is being
  eaten by crocodiles?

By means of his extremely
  slow metabolism he was
  enabled to keep far
  on the father light,
    far from the energy
    particle of the mother

Ah, it's a depressing situation:
  we imagine that
        we live and imagine
            that we die, too bad,
            too bad

Manly manly manly friend
  says the faggot on T V

CERRADA MEDELLIN BLUES

(FIRST SOLO)

1ST CHORUS

Even when I was a little boy
I was always alone
         with my guardian angel

Playing Tarzan
An icicle fell on me
     & cut my arm
I had a rope around my neck
I was hanged in Innifree
Had my hand cut off in Perfidee
Never had my fill
         of Thee

    ST MICHAEL IN THE CORNER,
       NINE FEET TALL

2ND CHORUS

   The Only One
      said Christ to me
When you're alone in Heaven
   with God
Who is my Father
       and Thine
You'll know that your self
     you
  And your guardian angel,
      One,
  And the self of any
Is
  The Only One—
  Sad Bent Head
    in "Cant-Get-Away
     From-That-Innisfree"

3RD CHORUS

I wonder what's hiding
    in the Cross?
 Did Jesus free the world?
 Before him there were murders
  officially.
 From body to effigy
   went history.
 Emily Dickinson me that,
   Thomas Hardy.
Roll me a pearl me
   that, O Big Sur Sea.
  And you, Ferlinghetti,
    how do you like that
  For rhyming free
  Free of a doctor's degree.
    Jean Louee.

4TH CHORUS

When I drink Bénédictine
I drink what the Holy
                    Father
                    Blessed
  I drink the blood of Christ?
        Naw!
    I drink Christ hisself—
    I say "Thank ye, God"
    and drink—
  And kiss the bottle
With the Cross on it
And D.O.M.
    the director of drinkers—
    The Heavenly Daiquiri?
    The troublesome Innisfree.

5TH CHORUS

What's all this Innisfree
    Running straight thru me?
Was Yeats invented it?
  Or O'Shawn the Yurner?
  Repetitive old rolling
     smoke balloons?
   Paul Newman's mouth
   with Spanish ladies
    arguing?
What?——Some truck?
Some cigaree?   Halles
  Market onions are free?
   My Guardian Angel's
   About to tell me—

6TH CHORUS

Alone with my Guardian Angel
  Alone in Innisfree
Alone in Mexico
        City
Alone with Benedict,
  Cave is free,
     alone is alone,
      Thou Only One—
  Alone and Alone
    The song of the pree
(Pree means prayer
 in English & Frenchie)
Choose yr words lightly,
    shit on the world,
  Merton'll die
    when he reads
       this from me

7TH CHORUS

I love Lax
 A regular Pax
  I love Lax
   not Ex Lax
   but
     you see
         Now Lax
  But's teeth ne'er held
 The comedian so grand
As them Lax horse teeth
 Held prayer
    to ground
Lax is a singer
  Lax is a goner
Lax is a gonna
  get mad onner

8TH CHORUS

My hand is moved
     by holy angels
  The life we are in
     is invisible
     Holy Ghost

If you could see me,
   hoodlum,
You'd be Saint
   Cant slash
     at a loser
  For Oy Yai O Paint
—Those lies are for liars
And me I'm a liar,
So liars forget
    the handsome beget
The ugliest pricks
   The angel beset

9TH CHORUS

But I stopped to think
  The angel dont care
  Nine feet tall
  Beside the wall
  Wants me cut out
  To do the rub out
But I got fathers to care for
Father Shoyer is one
Father Gioscia is two
  That's enough for you
      —Ah Lucien
  Al Jalisco
    Ah I'm drunk
      borracho

10TH CHORUS

Too drunk to write
Cant see the light

It's a strange thing when nuts
  get together
To form one cock—
   Young girls should shudder
     in that empty light—
  The holy of angels,
     I wonder what's he think?
  Shd push pencils
      for agers, masagers,
Masseurs and all?
  Oll?   Lovely bedoodlers
    in Time's Holy All
Holiest Ghostliest
  ramified Hall

11TH CHORUS

And, said I to the Angel,
that *shall* certainly do,
And the Angel said:
  D you remember Gregory?
Corso, the Way of Poetry?
    Orlovsky too?
      And Ginsberg O Shay?
      And Burroughs the Master
        speaks thru his teeth?
        And the writer of story
          the generous Honkey?
    And   Lafcadio the Holy
      Innocent of Russia,
    the Patriarch, & Sebastian?
    And Lucien?
      And Neal Cassady?

12TH CHORUS

Move my hand Lord
    move my hand
    Tell Ray Bremser
        something calm him
            down
    Tell Leroi Jones
        & Diane di Prima
                tooo
        They dont know
        that Heaven
        which is waiting for them
    In the land of OO

1ST CHORUS

"You can think by yourself"
        says God from Heaven
Talking to all 70 thousand
   Billion Four Thousand
   Eighty Two Trillions
   of Creatures in his Movie
. called "Creation"

        (pause)

2ND CHORUS

He means that all
those sentient beings
are free to think unimpeded
—Only God is the Only One
who knows that all the thinking
going on
is what the thinking going on

is thinking

And none of it ever happened

SHTMIMK!

Shtmimk?

3RD CHORUS

But like any other movie
  the thinking is gray
    but also big romances
    like Latin Love You music
    & all of it seems so golden
    steada gray.
  That's because it's a very strange
    movie
It is strange as dulcet gray.

 Hey looka me Ma
    I'm writing like Yorkshire
      Pudding De-Headed Gray
The proof is in the pudding
        they Bray
Just like any other old Canaday

4TH CHORUS

The brain is a pudding
   with raisins in't
Hey looka me Ma I'm thinking
  like Otay—
     Okay, Mémo,
     Está bien, Mémo,
      Parandero.

(That's what they mean Espanish
    'Hey kiddy, dont hit
     the bars too much,
      chico.'

Hey Baby dont yup at me
    in Azmetec!)

    Yair, Pard old Hoopard
     Hoomingway blew his head

      over Old I-day-o

5TH CHORUS

Hemingway Blues, is called.
Me too Blues—You Blues
—Thinkin Blues—Paris
Blues and Blacks—
Hurshy, move the tack!
Dont bring me no le-mon
    chiffin, pie, man,
      I'll break yore head in

Head already broken in
  No chin
    Yes chin
      Soft Chin
        Northport Autumn
        falling leaves blues
      And winter white
      sailboat philosopher
      blues, on sand,
Lois and Victor by name.

6TH CHORUS

All kindsa fine blues
　　even this minute
　　　in Vera Cruz,
　　　Terre Haute,
　　　Montana,
　　　　Golgotha,
　　　　　Heaven Door.

All kindsa information rattlin
　back & forth
　Crazy old angel midnight
　　world　talkin　singin
　　　rubbin　antennaes
　High on antenni
　　　and go Mondadori'n
　in Italy for to see sweep
　of Gary Venice Door's
　　Venetian oar

7TH CHORUS

Or go Atyastapafi'n
in other planets?
Goo, what a gaw!
And does wet boulders think?

I see the face of Christ
in the door
after it has been the face
of the Dog, the Owl,
the Lamb, the Lion,
Christ, the Dog again,
the Collie then suddenly
my God the Colleen!
Her soft brown eyes,
esperanza morena,
Then it's Christ again,
this time in profile
—This I just saw.

8TH CHORUS

I'm now going into a deep trance
  where I see visions—
Mwee hee hee ha ha.
    Johnny Holmes is just about
    the funniest man I know!
  He laughs in cemeteries
  in the woods of Connecticutt

(Connect ton cul, we used
             to call
           it
        in little
         Canada.)

Connect your arse.
  Some come on John, connect
  your arse to a Grave,
  pal, almost lover, and
    I'll bring ye sweet
     daydrids
    in the morning
  of the 2 thieves & Me

    & You

9TH CHORUS

(Written before I knew about Pascal —1965)

But John's like Pascal,
or like Frank O'hara even,
He wont let his head
Believe his heart
        & all that
So he skeptically adjusts
his glasses, leans forward eagerly,
 almost hugely,
      & roars

   Qui à poignez
     ton cul dans
      terre!

And 2 days later he looks it up
in a French Dictionary,
wondering what I'm thinking
about, and what I think
about him thinking.
Wow Very Strange

10TH CHORUS

It's dillier than that
they daisies they pud
in puddinhead blues.

To Earl of Shockshire:
"Sire, in this my Inscribe
May't you'll fee."
    The Earl of Shrockshire
    shires & showers & shh's
    on back a batch
        of Tanguipore
        Tangled
        Telegrams
    Mistaken by Saint Peter
    as Hair of the Gate

NOTES ON DATES AND SOURCES

"San Francisco Blues"
In a letter to Allen Ginsberg, Kerouac referred to writing this poem in March 1954, when he "left Neal's . . . and went to live in the Cameo Hotel on Third Street Frisco Skid Row."

"Richmond Hill Blues"
Written in Richmond Hill, New York, while Kerouac was living with his mother. He began the poem on September 4, 1953, and completed it later that month.

"Bowery Blues"
Kerouac dated the poem March 29, 1955.

"MacDougal Street Blues"
Kerouac dated the poem June 26, 1955.

"Desolation Blues"
  "Desolation Peak
   Mt. Baker Nat'l Forest
    Washington State
          August 1956"

"Orizaba 210 Blues"
  "Written in a tejado rooftop dobe cell
  at Orizaba 210, Mexico City, Fall 1956
  . . . by candlelight . . . "

"Orlanda Blues"
Begun in July 1957, finished February 17, 1958, this poem was written in Orlando, Florida—"Orlanda" in native parlance.

"Cerrada Medellin Blues"
   "July 1961
   37–A Cerrada Medellin
   Mexico, D.F., Mexico"
 Begun in June, finished in July.

Book of Blues is one of the unpublished manuscripts Jack Kerouac left in his meticulously organized archive. It does not contain all of Kerouac's unpublished blues poems—he chose not to include, for instance, "Berkeley Blues," "Brooklyn Bridge Blues," "Tangier Blues," "Washington DC Blues," and "Earthquake Blues." Comparisons with Kerouac's original handwritten notebooks indicate that in the process of editing the book he deleted and rearranged some verses, and made some small editorial changes. Readers familiar with the excerpts from "San Francisco Blues" published in *Scattered Poems* and the excerpts from "MacDougal Street Blues" published in *Heaven and Other Poems* will notice that Kerouac subsequently made changes in some of those verses. Kerouac's original typescript of *Book of Blues* is located in the Henry W. and Albert A. Berg Collection of English and American Literature, the New York Public Library, Astor, Lenox and Tilden Foundations.

I have taken the liberty of dedicating this book on Jack's behalf to two of his close friends and correspondents, Philip Whalen and Lew Welch.

—John Sampas,
Literary Executor, Estate of Jack and Stella Kerouac

JACK WOULD SPEAK THROUGH
THE IMPERFECT MEDIUM OF ALICE

So I'm an alcoholic Catholic mother-lover
yet there is no sweetish nectar no fuzzed-peach
thing no song sing but in the word
to which I'm starlessly unreachably faithful
you, pedant & you, politically righteous & you, alive
you think you can peal my sober word apart from my drunken
   word
my Buddhist word apart from my white sugar Thérèse word my
word to comrade from my word to my mother
but all my words are one word my lives one
my last to first wound round in finally fiberless crystalline skein

I began as a drunkard & ended as a child
I began as an ordinary cruel lover & ended as a boy who
                read radiant newsprint
I began physically embarrassing—"bloated"—&
                ended as a perfect black-haired laddy
I began unnaturally subservient to my mother &
                ended in the crib of her goldenness
I began in a fatal hemorrhage & ended in a
                tiny love's body perfect smallest one

But I began in a word & I ended in a word &
                I know that word better
Than any knows me or knows that word,
                probably, but I only asked to know it—
That word is the word when I say me bloated
                & when I say me manly it's
The word that word I write perfectly lovingly
                one & one after the other one

But you—you can only take it when it's that one & not
                   some other one,
Or you say "he lost it" as if I (I so nothinged) could ever
                   lose the word
But when there's only one word—when
                   you know them, the words—
The words are all only one word the perfect
                   word—
My body my alcohol my pain my death are only
                   the perfect word as I

Tell it to you, poor sweet categorizers
                   Listen
Every me I was & wrote
                   were only & all (gently)
That one perfect word

                                        —Alice Notley